1

VIEWS

By Jack Galmitz

Introduction By Beth Vieira

Views

copyright©2012 by Jack Galmitz

Seawall Press

VIEWS

By Jack Galmitz

Introduction By Beth Vieira

Views

Seawall Press

Table of Contents

Preview of *Views*

Preview of *Views*

A king has the blind men of the capital brought to the palace, where an elephant is brought in and they are asked to describe it.

"When the blind men had each felt a part of the elephant, the king went to each of them and said to each: 'Well, blind man, have you seen the elephant? Tell me, what sort of thing is an elephant?"

The men assert the elephant is either like a pot (the blind man who felt the elephant's head), a winnowing basket (ear), a plowshare (tusk), a plow (trunk), a granary (body), a pillar (foot), a mortar (back), a pestle (tail) or a brush (tip of the tail).

The men cannot agree with one another and come to blows over the question of what it is like and their dispute delights the king. The Buddha ends the story by comparing the blind men to preachers and scholars who are blind and ignorant and hold to their own views: *"Just so are these preachers and scholars holding various views blind and unseeing.... In their ignorance they are by nature quarrelsome, wrangling, and disputatious, each maintaining reality is thus and thus."* The Buddha then speaks the following verse:

O how they cling and wrangle, some who claim
  For preacher and monk the honored name!
For, quarreling, each to his view they cling.
Such folk see only one side of a thing.

(Udana, 68–69).

The Buddhist version of this Indian parable turns the blindness of the men into something metaphoric about how they cling to their views without seeing where they stand and how that stance works in relation to others who also have views. The Jain version, which concludes that all the blind men are correct, promotes a kind of knowledge that might be called "weak relativism," where views are equally valid no matter how much they conflict with each other. The Buddhist version of the story might be called "strong relativism" for contrast because the problem is seeing "only one side of a thing" and taking that as the whole. The tale, an admonition against sectarian views, implicitly suggests that if the men stopped clinging to their own views and cooperated instead, they might come closer to seeing more of the elephant, in a sense overcoming their own blindness.

The task of layering and corroborating views, though laborious and communal (perhaps never complete), is a form of strong relativism that Nietzsche called "perspectivism." Though not developed as a systematic epistemology, it, like interpretation, is privileged in Nietzsche's approach:

> There is only a perspectival seeing, only a perspectival "knowing"; and the more affects we allow to speak about a matter, the more eyes, different eyes, we know how to bring to bear on one and the same matter, that much more complete will our "concept" of this matter, our "objectivity" be. (Friedrich Nietzsche, *On the Genealogy of Morality: A Polemic.* trans. Maudemarie Clarke and Alan J. Swenswen. Indianapolis: Hackett Publishing, 1998.)

Views, the collection of work by Jack Galmitz, shows the power of allowing perspectival seeing, the layering of views, to accumulate on a topic that might be a bit like an elephant in miniature—contemporary haiku. Like the blind men in the parable, people cling to their own views of haiku even though they have grasped just a part. Galmitz in tandem with fourteen poets follows Nietzsche's lead to allow "more affects...more eyes" to the matter.

Through interviews, book reviews, and critical pieces, Galmitz covers the poetry and larger concerns of a broad range of writers: paul m., Peter Yovu, Chris Gordon, John Martone, Ban'ya Natsuishi, Tateo Fukutomi, Tohta Kaneko, Robert Boldman, Marlene Mountain, Grant Hackett, Richard Gilbert, Dimitar Anakiev, Mark Truscott, and Fay Aoyagi. Each writer appears in exquisite specificity, as if Galmitz can disappear into each's shadow and yet at the same time be so active that he pulls them into the spotlight to take a fine-tuned look at the work each does.

As in Nietzsche's perspectivism, there is no forced effort to systematize the results. Galmitz resists trying to define or categorize via abstraction, and instead he moves along with each poet to focus on minute details as well as broad concerns, a combination appropriate for the genre of haiku. Even the very notion of what the genre of haiku is, too often taken for granted, is actually up for examination and questioning. For the most part, more traditional definitions of haiku are left by the wayside as rule-bound and restrictive rather than generative and expansive.

But that might be too simple a way to put it. Rather it is clear that relinquishing a pre-conceived idea about haiku outside of the actual work of active writers, who come close to grappling with that very question in almost every poem, produces a fuller picture. It is left to the reader to take up the layering of these views and see haiku as a living and changing practice pursued by a variety of artists.

One way Galmitz characterizes what poets do is to invoke Wittgenstein's notion of "language games." In part, the idea of language games was formulated to account for non-referential, definition-resistant tendencies in language. Language games account for multiplicity, lack of fixedness, and use or activity, where meaning is analogous to a move in a game.

And Galmitz shows again and again how to be a good player, willing to travel with the word's uses through "a complicated network of similarities, overlapping, and crisscrossing" (Wittgenstein, *Philosophical Investigations, 66*). In many cases, we see him in between words, examining the spaces that define the lines of poetry, or parts of language such as dashes and letters in what Blake would call the "minute particulars" of creative labor.

Galmitz explores the effects of breaking up language with poems such as this one by John Martone:

winter
coat
& gloves
he's
an
other
sparrow

Like other lineation effects, this poem creates multiple meanings. Here the deliberate lack of a hyphen produces the word "other," which might be said to stand for the possibility of othering not only in this particular poem but in each of the poems that focus on the slippage created by the concrete layout of the lines.

Attention to this level of creative labor not only gives us a strong sense of each poet; it also gives us what Tohta Kaneko calls *"shiso"* or "existentially embodied thinking." As Galmitz explains in "The Romance of Primitivism," the term is related to, yet also opposed to, an emptier concept of ideology. Whether it is the experience of the poet represented in the poem or the experience of the poem as represented by the poet, embodiment figures in these essays as part of the creative labor of the language game.

We can see embodiment from a concern with the form of the poem on the page. This concern is especially critical in concrete poetry, where the shapes of the words on the page are resonant with the way meaning emerges. Minimalist Mark

Truscott gives us one of the many poems that plays with the effects of concrete poetry:

SQUARE
which is
which is

The repetition in the poem calls forward what might be called the iterative effect of language, an effect seen in other forms in several of the poets.

For instance, Chris Gordon creates serial poems, all with a repeating line. Three series are looked at carefully: Invisible Circus, Chinese Astronauts, and the Crow. Two examples from Invisible Circus show the delightful language game created by Gordon's serial approach:

Your watch stopped when
You bought your ticket to
The Invisible Circus

The Invisible Circus
Goes from town to town
Never really moves

Gordon's own off-the-cuff remark, "*Caveat emptor*: Don't go to the Invisible Circus!" playfully cautions the reader to be alert, for as the investigation of the poetry goes on, we see the workings of the unconscious. As the title of the piece suggests, even the quotidian is superlative.

Repetition figures in a different way in the monostichs of Grant Hackett:

The spirit of the bell delivers a cry : : I stare into this world without peace
The spirit of the bell delivers a cry (I stare into this world without peace)
The spirit of the bell (I stare into this world) delivers a cry (without peace)

Hackett calls these transformations "Innerweavings," which Galmitz connects to one-line haiku poetry and also demonstrates the way the lines open up to possibilities that reject closure.

The visceral effects of language in repetition are just a few ways that some of the poets deploy embodied thinking. Even though there are points of overlap among the poets, as there would be in any language game, the poets take up these techniques for different effects and with different backgrounds. The tension

12

inherent in written language between the visual and aural poles comes into play in many of the poems.

"Typology & Poetry: Richard Gilbert Experiments" pulls this concern to the foreground with close readings of poems such as this one:

a drowning man

             p
     u
     l
     l
     e
     d

     i
     n
     t
     o

     v
     i
     o
     l
     e
     t

     w
     o
     r
     l
     d
     s

             g
     r
     a
     s
     p
     i
     n
     g

     h
     y

```
d
r
a
n
g
e
a
```

A striking poem made all the more elusive by the typographical layout, which has
the effect of slowing us down so that we almost gurgle out the letters as if we too are
drowning.

At the same time we have poets like Peter Yovu, who, even though he makes
use of the visual effects, admits that he prefers to read poems aloud. So at the aural
pole we have poems like this:

> mosquito she too
> insisting insisting she
> is is is is is

Though delightfully onomatopoetic, Yovu pushes the effects of sound in language, in
Galmitz's words, as "somewhat dissociated from its meaning." An example of this
dissociative effect is the following poem:

> millionating beast
> quadramillion hooves
> drum down the groundskin

The poet creates neologisms to carry a large part of the effect of the poem through
sound.

Sometimes when we follow these pathways into the poetry, the language
games take over and leave the players without clear-cut agency over what they are
doing, either as poets or interpreters. Instead of a sense of loss of control, these
moments are presented as exhilarating, for they let in something larger, whether
the unconscious, multiplicity, or a set of specific concerns (social, political, spiritual,
natural). For instance, paul m. emphasizes how the creative process takes over: "I
allow myself the freedom to follow the poem, and let it dictate its own structure."

The lack of uncertainty and multiplicity of meanings celebrated in this
collection brings us back to the power of taking a perspectival approach, one that
layers differing views. One of the central interpretive concepts might be best

represented by the word *aporia*. From a Greek word that means "impasse," *aporia* has been used by such post-modernists as Jacques Derrida, Paul de Man, and Luce Irigaray in close textual readings to show a key moment of indeterminacy that usually results not just in a layering of meanings but in the impossibility of making a determination. More radical than poetic ambiguity, *aporia* throws into question how meaning is made in the first place, again an uncertainty that is welcomed with exhilaration rather than a sense of loss. In a reading of a poem by Richard Gilbert, Galmitz concludes that again we encounter "an example of poetry as highlighting *aporia* as its central purpose; its playing with the deficiencies of language as its starting and ending point."

Though Galmitz does not claim that each poet is self-consciously post-modern, he does use post-modern thought to examine the poetry and to characterize the contemporary language game of haiku-informed writing. Jean-François Lyotard makes several appearances in *Views* as one of the influential post-modern theorists. Lyotard advances a notion of "metanarratives" that are quasi-mythological beliefs about human purpose, human reason, and human progress—parts of Modernism that are challenged by post-modern discourse. Lyotard in fact suggests that a pragmatic approach to experimentation and diversity be assessed in the context of language games, which is precisely what Galmitz seeks to do in *Views*.

So far we concentrated largely on the formal properties of poetry though as we've seen a lot more is at stake, especially about language and meaning. Post-modernist thought challenges many assumptions that might be taken for granted not only about language and meaning. Three topics stand out in this collection: nature, politics, and subjectivity. Though the topics overlap, each can be held up for partial viewing, often with the unexpected effect of *aporia* when it comes to an attempt to make definitive declarations.

Nature might be the most fraught topic since it is of course the most naturalized. This problem is compounded by assumptions about the genre of haiku, that it is a form of "nature poetry," with the tradition of using seasonal words, *kigo*, as well as descriptions of nature. These assumptions are taken on directly by Tohta Kaneko with a surprising revelation: the idea of an objective sketch attributed to Masaoka Shiki and then imported as a formative concept for Western haiku is actually based on a complete misunderstanding. While true that Shiki used *shasei*, "sketch," it was actually a student, Takaham Kyoshi, who advocated something "objective," which Kaneko calls "obedience to nature," to the poetry of "birds and flowers." Furthermore, Kaneko points to the "corrupting influence of modernism, insofar as it separates man from nature, sets them at strife." He instead uses the category *ikimono*, "living beings" in a way that allows for a less restrictive view.

It's important to let Kaneko's point sink in since the misunderstanding he foregrounds has influenced so many Western haiku writers. Though paul m. at first seems to align himself with a more traditional view, his interaction with Galmitz in his interview leaves us with something more complex. In relation to the "veneration for the venerable age of the universe," Galmitz playfully calls paul "a man with a visa," which captures what the title of the essay seeks to catch in "discarding the dividing line" between subject and object. Somewhat outside as a visitor, but allowed permission with a visa, paul m. can produce poems with or without explicit reference to himself, where the reader still feels the qualities of the poet.

> small plot of land
> the same sun
> I was born under

> sun on the horizon
> who first
> picked up a stone

Both poems can be said to line up with acts of veneration, and yet there is also the voice of questioning: both who am I? and who are we? The first question arises from the contrasts of huge expanses of space and time and the smaller awareness attributed to the "I." In the second poem, another ageless question hints at potential for destruction and aggression, a thing all living things share. Galmitz characterizes paul m. as "not only a man 'in' the world, but a man within which is the world." Not only does it address what may be a false dividing line, but it may be the most beautiful distillation of what it means to be an artist.

Though this description is far removed from a moment at which paul recites one of Galmitz's poems, for me it echoes at this very moment.

> Inside of me
> Bison are stampeding
> Across the caves

The bison are simultaneously natural creatures, wild and furious, and yet they are art, the famous cave paintings. Whether out of veneration or violence or a combination of both, that primordial moment of the creation of art moves not just in caves but also through the poet, whose "inside" echoes the container of the caves. Galmitz is also "a man within which is the world."

"The world should not lie useless. It should be scooped up in the hands and sifted through the fingers and scored with the ridges of the palm." This sentence introduces his essay, "The Cultivated Field: Tateo Fukutomi's *Straw Hat*." Cultivation, what we do with nature, brings new worlds into being, not without memory of the old.

In a field
where buried axe-heads surface
tree spirits assemble

At such intersections, Galmitz muses, "we find our responsibility." And yet this sense of awareness is not overly moralized. In fact, similar to cultivation, it is a process that takes continuous labor and attention, even in the face of great odds:

Memory of the atomic bomb
every time the wind pulls off my hat
I put it back on

While Galmitz calls this haiku tragi-comic, it also emphasizes the action involved in cultivation, something that requires constant attention and repetitive action, here in cycles of memory, like that of the fields. But the wind blows in both places.

Cultivation of nature in the form of domination is just the beginning of the view of Dimitar Anakiev's work. Galmitz highlights a speech by Anakiev in which "capitalist haiku" is called out. This type of haiku turns out to be "dominated by dehumanized topics of nature." With some help from such neo-Marxist writers as Theodore Adorno, we get a clearer picture not only of the domination of nature but also of the actual separation of human from nature as ideological results. Later in the piece, we see how the human use of nature for ideological purposes is deeply embedded in the politics of war for Anakiev:

In the Balkans
at the calling out of "rustic"
swastikas sprout

The rural areas are not merely "rustic." They are where the far-right thrives on the basis of what Anakiev calls "goat's milk" philosophy, which symbolizes connection not only to the land but also to an ideology.

A doctor as well as a film-maker and poet, Anakiev became one of the "Erased" during the war, a whole group deprived of identity, civil rights, passports, and respect. It is no accident then that the most passionate calls for politics in haiku come from Anakiev, both in his statements and in his poetry itself.

> A big field of
> cultural struggle: hens
> are laying eggs again

Cultural struggle engages the poet in the social and political worlds that he already inhabits and is witness to. Galmitz turns to Adrienne Rich, who has called for poetry to take on its role as a social practice and to articulate the language of public pain. The poems of Anakiev serve not only as testimony to his own experience, but they serve a project of cultural memory for the war in the Balkans and also for World War II with German domination.

> Mittleeuropa:
> in the grey cloud
> a shadow of death

It is hardly surprising that Anakiev finds excitement in Richard Gilbert's *Poems of Consciousness* in the development of "international haiku," something that embraces democracy and resists authority.

"Haiku as a protest" is shared by the poet Marlene Mountain as a partial summary of her life's work. Experimentation with the form and use of techniques like cut-up and crosswords is a strong feature of her work. But it is as a unique voice in feminist politics that underwrites so much of what she does. Mountain seems to create her own woman-centered language because it is clear that even language is not gender neutral:

> thousands of women gather and talk in spite of language

To give a sense of how Mountain works with and against language to carve out a feminist politics, Galmitz cites this sequence from "womancrativa":

> i am no beginning i am no end
>
> i am chaoscoswommos
>
> from my womwomb all is
>
> from my gynitals all flows

birth of wom harvest of wom

shesharing I will make myself into ourselves

sheyes again I will shegive a big birth

When challenged in an interview about her insistence on feminist politics and throwing haiku into the political realm, she gives this tongue-in-cheek response: "Haiku can be a lot more than pears and yellow windows." And she finally answers by explaining that she is not "stressing the political" but rather "recognizing its existence."

A moment of particular interest occurs when Galmitz reproduces a letter by Haruo Shirane, author of the magisterial study on Basho, *Traces of Dreams*. Shirane writes of Mountain's work, "Great poets don't stick to the rules; they make their own. You belong in that company." He adds that "constantly seeking new horizons, new words, new emotions" is constitutive of the "haikai spirit."

Since, as the saying goes, "the personal is the political," I want to turn next to the topic of subjectivity and the "new horizons, new words, new emotions" found there in so much of the work of *Views*. Any traditional notion of a "self" that is in complete self-possession and is self-creating and self-sufficient is undermined throughout the collection, whether by post-modern challenges to the production of this kind of subjectivity or by recourse to "othering" in language that takes the form of explicit references to psychology.

Galmitz uses the notion of an archetype, that of the Trickster of Native American mythology, to show the workings of the serial poem on the Crow by Chris Gordon:

a last few tricks ask the crow

a second glance at your wife the crow

cheats at love but not at cards the crow

Galmitz shows that the Trickster in the figure of the crow "transmutes the quotidian and thereby aids us in keeping alive." And true to the effects of the unconscious, Gordon cannot say definitively whether he is using the archetype or not. The unconscious figures prominently as the uncanny in Gordon's series on the

Invisible Circus and as part of the surrealist irrational in the monostichs of Grant Hackett.

These concerns all come to the forefront in the final essay of *Views,* "*Jouissance*: The Poetic Achievement of Fay Aoyagi." Galmitz uses two difficult post-modern theorists, Lyotard and Lacan, to read Aoyagi's book, *Beyond the Reach of My Chopsticks.* "*Jouissance*" is a critical term in Lacanian psychoanalysis. It pokes a little fun at the limited sexuality that Freud proposed in his drive theory since the release of tensions of that drive is only a crude version of the enjoyment and types of desire expressed by *jouissance.*

Galmitz starts with the sense of loss that challenges this *jouissance.* In a haiku that lends itself to the title of the collection, Aoyagi writes

low winter moon
just beyond the reach
of my chopsticks

Galmitz ends a multi-faceted reading of the poem with this statement: "The ensemble of words may also refer to what exists just beyond her Japanese utensils, the world of the Other, as she is now in America, a foreign country." Loss sets in motion the workings of desire, which is attached to objects that Lacan describes as the "little other" and the "big Other."

Galmitz traces the workings of the unconscious from dark associations to this delightful one:

summer's end
I trade my wings
for fins

A moment of playful undifferentiation mimics the childlike world Lacan calls the Imaginary. But lurking all around these moments are the losses that accentuate them as precious. And poems often convey this loss in the form of lack or longing:

my yearning to spend a night inside a tulip magnolia

Though the poems of Aoyagi are intimate, she, like Anakiev, has the world of a war-torn nation lingering in her mind, with poems on the atomic bombs of Nagasaki and Hiroshima.

Nagasaki Anniversary
the constellation
we could never see from here

Hiroshima Day—
I lean into the heat
of the stone wall

These losses are also "just beyond the reach of my chopsticks."

Galmitz tracks a kind of development in which Aoyagi "matures into an awareness not only of the importance of existents other than her own, but to the fact that loss is ineluctable, that memory sustains, that 'selves' that once were are now recognized as merely masks."

Halloween—
I dress as the self
I left somewhere

The striking part of this realization, as evidenced in the Halloween poem, is that it remains relatively untroubled. Perhaps this is because the particular subjectivity presented here is only momentarily attached to little objects of desire and can instead see these attachments from the perspective of the Other. Galmitz describes a moment of *jouissance* as "a love that is never satisfied for an unattainable, uncircumscribed object," about this poem:

a "forever stamp" on a letter to the ocean

Here Aoyagi might be articulating what it means to be a writer, its exhilarations along with its impossibilities, all sealed together in this message-in-a-bottle haiku.

The challenges that face the writers are shared by the readers who receive these smallest of poems and attempt to decipher meanings inscribed on "a letter to the ocean." Luckily, the reader is guided by the openness and imagination of Jack Galmitz, who shows us how to play the language games of the poets and not foreclose on possibilities like the blind men with the elephant. The fourteen pieces that make up this collection of views demonstrate the power of allowing perspectival seeing to give us layerings of meaning rather than one singular message.

Beth Viera
Santa Cruz, California
April 2012s

Interviews

Discard the Dividing Line: Conversing with paul m.

JG: Hi, Paul. Welcome to Roadrunner Haiku Journal.

pm: Glad to be here, Jack. Thanks for having me.

JG: Congratulations on the publication of your latest book, <u>a few days north days few</u> (Redmoon Press, 2011); it's quite a compelling body of work and your original linocuts compliment it. I find the linocuts resemble the poems: both carefully strip away everything except what you want to stand out and both have a simplicity that culminates from sophistication. Do you find a similarity in the two practices?

pm: That's an interesting observation. However I'm not sure the end result of either is as premeditated as you make it sound. Peter Yovu once wrote that a haiku "is a balance between control and surrender." I think that is a key concept of any creative act. An experienced poet is really just an observant poet, meaning that at all times they have twenty kigo in their head—what is representative around/within them at that moment—and that the rest of the poem is their reaction to that representation. A kigo is simply the bedrock we all share, and each poet leaps from it. I think we have control over that first part in the sense that we understand it, but we can be surprised by the leap. Regarding the illustrations, I had definitive ideas of what I wanted the picture to look like, but so much of "getting to the end result" was outside my control—whether it was my lack of skill, or the surprise that what I thought would hold ink didn't. But both creative acts clearly work that balance.

JG: Speaking of control and surrender, you have certainly been influenced by the naturalist, John Muir. But, I sense an equal impact in your work from the American Transcendentalists. For instance, your first poem

              with eyes closed spring grass

reminds me of Walt Whitman's "I lean and loafe at my ease, observing a spear of summer grass." And your assiduous searching for happenings in the natural world reminds me of Henry David Thoreau's remarks that "we must learn to ...keep ourselves awake, not by mechanical aids, but by an infinite expectation of the dawn"; and his view that to "transact some private business...to trade with the Celestial Empire," which was Nature, would elevate his soul. The universe, for the Transcendentalists, was akin to Richard Bucke's <u>Cosmic Consciousness.</u> Would you agree that your influences can be traced to these forebears?

pm: Very much so. That's a great quote from Thoreau, conscious as he was of life's continuous creation. As a child of the Los Angeles suburbs and then as a resident of San Francisco for a number of years, I have always felt that half of the world was missing. That half I discovered in Nature. So I make time to get out into it, to see its relationships, and to see what it can teach me about its larger self, including myself. I am hesitant (I'm an accountant after all) to extend those mysteries to the larger cosmic consciousness Bucke speaks of, but the writings of the transcendentalists have helped me steer my own thoughts. Interestingly, Dee Evetts in an issue of

Frogpond once asked the haiku community why so many poems were written about nature when so many of the poets lived in cities. I answered that cities are static and lacked seasons, and in turn our relationship to the changing seasons. Life is change. It is Thoreau's 'dawn.' And I'd argue that humans have a seasonal clock. I don't think it's a coincidence that the natural world mimics our emotional lifetime. JG: Paul, your haiku for the most part are written in the classical mode: a "seasonal reference," followed by a pause or cut, and followed by complimentary or contrary elements. For me, this is reminiscent of Thoreau's admonition "I say beware of all enterprises that require new clothes, and not rather a new wearer of clothes." Your choice of a traditional form for your haiku also reminds me of other spiritual heritages-particularly the Amish and Chasidim-who choose simple black suits, because this is suitable for the conventional world and releases the wearer's intellectual energy to devote to higher purposes. Your formatting also reminds me somewhat again of Thoreau's hut at Walden; if you recall he borrowed an ax, bought and re-used some boards from another house, and otherwise used materials available from his natural environment. I think we can definitely see in one of your poems how you build from heritage and what's readily available:

> sparrow song
> a fence built
> of found logs

You have included in your volume some experimental haiku, which I'll get to later. But for now, I wonder how you respond to my above analysis of your preference for tradition.

pm: There was a year recently in which I was very worried that the repetitiveness of the form would become tiresome, and looked to writers like John Martone to see how I could vary what you call the 'classical' three-line structure, to open up a poem mid-line or mid-word (something he does very interestingly) to create misreadings and extra-readings. But ultimately I decided that such misreadings were things to be used sparingly, since in most cases I am trying to share a particular moment, and those misreadings draw too much attention to themselves. Perhaps the choice of picture over frame? Yet, while I do write the majority of my poems in the 'classical' structure, I allow myself the freedom to follow the poem, and let it dictate its own structure—whether three line, one line, or many. I suspect all writers go through that struggle with form, especially a form like haiku which we (correctly or incorrectly) inherited.

JG: Well, I find your forms virtuous- pleasing and balanced. I do not think they slip into the weaknesses that a predetermined format for a poem might tend: repetition, imitation, even self-imitation, numbing of the sensitivities. In fact, my overall impression of your poems is that they convey virtue as a moral character, a human characteristic, and they achieve this because of your engagement in your subjects, but more of this later. I'd like to take a look first at the few experimental haiku that you include in your volume. The first one I'd like to look at was published previously in Roadrunner:

outdated magazines
In the green room
Of a rose

I remember reading it, liking it, but not quite grasping it. Now that I've had more time to examine it, I think it creatively captures the green sepals opening and separating as the rose matures; what was initially fresh, fragrant, even a bit glossy-the sepals-containing all that was new, as magazines are when shiny and contain the latest information, become outworn and exist in a separate space-room- at the presence of the flower. I think the poem uses metaphor quite powerfully.

Rather than discuss the pros and cons of metaphor in haiku-once frowned upon-I would point to the wonderful, excited reception the Japanese haijin had to the haiku of Tomas Transtromer and its use of metaphor as reported by Kaj Falkman in his Homage to Tomas Transtromer in Japan, which can be found at Troutswirl at the Haiku Foundation website.

Before moving on to some other examples of your experimental haiku, how did you feel when you wrote what would be called a post-modernist haiku?

pm: A short answer would be that I felt 'excited!' As evident by their sparse number in the book, they are something I'm still working out. In the last few years we've seen an explosion of exciting non-traditional haiku at the periphery of the community, some similar to Japanese gendai work, but often more of an abstract style that is definitely American. One of the first such poems I saw was your own 'Inside of me / Bison are stampeding / Across caves' which remains today one of my favorite haiku of all-time. I think my poem works in a similar way, although I am hesitant to explain it since logical summations distort its more organic genesis. The poem plays with the idea of a 'green room' which is traditionally a room stage performers wait in before they go on stage. I had in mind the green room of the Tonight Show or Letterman with their true and pseudo celebrities. The final line makes the imaginative leap (a haiku-leap, if you will) to the room being the calyx of a rose, only now the rose has faded—much like all celebrity will. In reality the tight bud was perceived first and I imagined what might be inside.

JG: The second experimental haiku I'd like to examine is the following:

a line borrowed
from another poet
spring rain

What I find engaging about this poem is the fact that the subject is never really disclosed, although when read another way it is: literally, the poet admits borrowing a line while it is raining outside in spring. Of course, read differently, the facticity of "spring rain" is the borrowed line. This poem operates by ambiguity, a poetic device that's been highly valued in mainstream poetry since the 1950s. Another poem that works with ambiguity is also a concrete poem: it is spread out on two pages, and the ambiguity arises from the fact that the poems on each page can be read as separate poems, until the reader realizes it is a concrete poem and is actually one poem dragged across two pages:

white wood asters a thousand   years the lake

Again, ambiguity, as here, is always surprising and so stirring, and the images on
the first page are powerfully drawn. Then, in addition, once I realized it was one
poem, the long gap, the separation of the poem's parts on two pages, strengthens
the number of years it takes for the transformation of a lake into a forest.
Then, there's another haiku that would be called a concrete poem:

> all night
> thud of
> ripe apples
> at the
> u
> &
> l
> verse's
> core

I find the separations of stanzas strategic and strong in this haiku. "all night"
implies the length of intimacy between the u and I; the sound of the lovers is
natural and comes without control-a "thud", the way "ripe apples," young lovers
together do, and I appreciate the reverberation of the word "core" to describe the
center of the experience as it reconnects to "ripe apples."

My question to you Paul is do you have a different regard for these experimental
haiku than for your more formalistic haiku?

pm: That's an interesting question, and a little like asking a parent who their
favorite child is—the one who asks endless questions (especially ones you don't have
the answer to) or the quiet one who breaks windows which inadvertently lets in
birdsong? You learn from both. These particular poems presented something that I
couldn't resist. The poem "white wood asters" was originally a one-liner to mimic
the surface of the lake, and it wasn't until I started placing the poem on the page
that I saw how moving its parts could heighten its effect. I'll go back to my earlier
comment that I allow myself the freedom to follow the poem where it wants to lead.
Each individual poem has a 'feel' for when it is done. A trope in haiku is that we
want to leave preconception aside to approach our subjects openly and honestly.
That applies to form as well. I'm delighted you recognized "all night" as a haiku,
which I definitely consider it to be. That poem in particular begged to be broken
apart to create interesting readings. The phrase "u / & / I" (you and I) and "verse"
from the original word "universe" would never have risen to the surface without
opening it up. That's a poem I won't say more about other than I find it very
dynamic. It's a favorite.

JG: As I mentioned earlier, Paul, I consider your forms as vessels for virtues, in the
sense of morality, as a human characteristic. I'd like to start this discussion with
the oldest, that is, your veneration for the venerable age of the universe and your
place in it as "a visitor myself," as a man with a visa so to speak, or as you
emphasize it in part of the title of your book "days few." Here are some poems
illustrating this:

small plot of land
the same sun
I was born under

sequoia that fell
long before my birth
the path around it

sun on the horizon
who first
picked up a stone

ancient moon
an outgoing wave
reveals sand crab holes

Your choice of such phrases as "small plot of land," which may either refer to earth itself or even to you; "the path around it," as perhaps humanities small patch of space in the ancient and huge universe; the beginnings of things in "sun on the horizon," and our ancestral beginnings and history of aggression and violence; and your well-chosen adjective "ancient" for the moon in contradistinction to the small recent lives of mole crabs; all of this reveals your humility here in the universe. Is the sense of being small and short-lived in the universe the primary source of your veneration?

pm: I'm going to use a definition of 'veneration' that means "respect and awe" of which I have plenty for the universe. I'm also going to put a footnote on mankind's "history of aggression and violence": the universe is a plenty violent place on its own. But I am astonished by mankind's Dark Age claim, and in many ways our contemporary selfish insistence, that we are the center of the universe—or even of this planet. The universe is an unknowably huge and complicated place, and the more we look outward, or even inward, regarding our physical presence here and now, we prove time and again that we are really quite insignificant. And in the face of it, quite fragile. While I had recognized that fact in certain poems I hadn't seen that as a larger theme of my poetry, but upon reflection it certainly is one. "A man with a visa" well describes my feelings—and perhaps us all. I think your question brings up an interesting point about poetry, especially haiku (if you'll forgive the sidebar). If we want to write honest poems, and view the world honestly, we speak about leaving preconception aside when we approach our subjects. But that's a two way street. If we are truly open in our confrontation with the world as it is we bring into the moment our true selves as well. Basho admonished us to go to the pine to learn of the pine. But in the process we don't just learn the 'true' meaning of the pine; we also learn the 'true' meaning of ourselves.

JG: While it's not unprecedented in haiku, your inclusion of the darker side of nature-the struggle to survive, mortality-gives rise to the virtue of compassion in your work. Here are a few examples:

> returning geese
> her ashes still
> in the plain tin

> spring morning
> flies return
> to a crab carcass

> stern wind
> the branch an osprey
> adds to its nest

> three new planets
> the bitter roe
> of a sea urchin

> farewell walk
> a stretch of shore
> known for driftwood

Did compassion develop in you over the years as a result of observation of nature, or was compassion a quality you already possessed, but was perhaps enhanced by your practice of haiku?

pm: I don't know that you can honestly interact with the world and not gain more compassion—either through the practice of poetry, the observation of animals, or simply shopping in a store. Whether I already possessed it is a question for my mother, but I suspect you know the answer she'll give. I mentioned that the universe was a violent place on its own. I do see some poetry, haiku included, that seems to want to veer from that seeing, to only present the beautiful and uplifting, which I find false and a bit cowardly. The world is a complicated and messy place. If we are going to value honesty in poetry we need to represent all that we see.

JG: There is also a generosity in your haiku, Paul, that testifies to your willingness to share the world and your belief that there is room for all things in it. While this is trait of haiku, I find it markedly so in your work.

> hand in hand
> room enough
> for each star

> no voice
> but for the stones
> autumn brook

blue shadows
deep into the snow
split-hoof of a deer

a brook
with a name...
dancing mayflies

These are just a sample of the many instances in your book where you make way for
existents in the world, appreciate them for what they are, do homage to life in its
variegated forms, show respect, which is generosity of spirit. Having said this, I
wonder if you think that the practice of haiku can create by constantly practicing it,
generosity and respect beyond the confines of the page and into the world?
pm: I am reluctant to assign that kind of power to poetry, but I will add that I would
hope so, but no more so than other literature or music or anything else that is
shared between people. I wrote in the introduction to this book that "I believe that
we don't share poetry to revel in our differences, but rather to seek comfort in our
similarities." I realize that people often approach haiku for its exoticness, its
cultural 'otherness'; yet I believe people are essentially the same everywhere, and
love and fear the same things. After a time—especially after being exposed to other
cultures' arts—that desire for exoticness is hopefully replaced with a recognition of
that fact.
JG: Paul, regardless of the fact that you write haiku in the traditional style, there is
something uncommon, distinctive about your work. I can literally feel your
engagement in each poem, your participation as observer/creator, so much so that I
would say you are not only a man "in" the world, but a man within which is the
world. I feel in your works the common divide between subject and object, self and
non-self is discarded and no such dividing line exists. The Zen Buddhist monk and
writer Thich Nhat Hanh calls such a state of being "inter-being," or interpenetration, or co-dependent origination. Few would argue that opposites, the
whole range of them, are not contingent upon one another, not defined by one
another, but can exist independently. This is not only ancient wisdom, but wisdom
shared by modern psychology/psychoanalysis, , modern science in general.
So, though you write classical haiku, you are still modern. As Jorge Luis Borges
put it in his book This Craft Of Verse (Harvard University Press, 2000) "we are
modern by the very simple fact that we live in the present... We are modern
whether we want to be or not."
The question remains how you achieve this state of inter-being and I would venture
to say that it is because of your intense observation, love, involvement in your work
and subjects that this comes about. And, this in turn, derives from your vigorous,
exacting craft of the use of language. I'll show you what I consider some of the more
telling examples.

> river of stars
> a burning stick
> from a neighboring fire

Here we have hermeticism: that which is below corresponds to that which is above...to accomplish the miracle of the One Thing. The divine sparks and the camping sparks: there's a sense of community, and though there is no ostensible witness, the poet as crafter is what I call man as metaphor maker, the actual joiner of above and below. Or here:

> early dusk...
> an inch of snow
> on a half inch branch

Though the poem works on the literal level and seems perfectly objective, there is also the metaphoric at play, the slow progress of dusk, spreading beyond the confines of things of the world, larger than them in size, in reach. Again, though the author is literally absent, the world is understood through its migration and transformation through him. Or this:

> ring around the moon
> the broken face
> of a tidal berm

Again, the comparison of the halo round the moon to the elevated berm above the backshore, both round, both with implied faces, is the world as created by the poet, with assonance and consonance both holding the edifice in place, joining it, serves well to illustrate how as a poet you don't merely present images to evoke a mood, but actively create further meaning through association. Or here,

> rib shadows
> on a loping coyote
> a field of cut hay

> river in flood-
> from low brush
> a second moose calf

These two poems you set on the same page. The one, a starving, perishing coyote, the second another new calf, new life. We would not know the state of the coyote if the author did not give us words like "rib shadows" and compare them to "cut hay," or would we fully feel the impact of starvation without the rising "flood" of the river and its metaphoric relationship to bursting second (additional) life in the birth of the "calf."

In these poems, and throughout the entire book, we can feel the presence of an author, an author who is complex, dedicated, sophisticated, gentle, compassionate, aware always and attentive to the smallest of details. How do you regard your energetic engagement with the world as envisioned in your poems, Paul?

pm: Thank you for your kind appreciation of my work. To answer your question, while I'm not overtly conscious of the activity, I can only say that I hope I show the interdependence/interpenetration of things that you say. The world is a large and complex place. And I'll add, a messy one. You are right that I feel life is short, fragile, and that I am but a "man with a visa." I think if I didn't try to anchor myself to it somehow I'd get lost, the way ancient sailors feared falling off the edge of the world. For me the only way to get that anchor is by engagement. You can't hide yourself in a cloister. Yet despite the world's messiness, it is filled with great wonder, so it is a joy to engage. In my poetic journey (which is just a fancy way of saying how I've changed and hopefully grown as a poet over the years) I've picked up advice from a number of very sharp people. Fay Aoyagi, in the introduction to her first collection Chrysanthemum Love, famously wrote "I don't write haiku to report the weather. I write to tell my stories." That's an idea I carry with me. So when I use a kigo to anchor myself to this world, such as 'winter sun', it isn't just to tell you that it's winter and the sun is shining, but also to ask you to feel the chill in the air, your hands warm in your pockets, perhaps collar turned up against a bracing wind, yet also feeling worn down by the length of another long year, perhaps thoughts of mortality... and that the sun is shining weakly through the bare branches of a tree—because that's what I was experiencing when I wrote the poem. The haiku is a short poem, possibly the shortest, and it needs all the help it can get to impart information to the reader. That's why I use kigo, as a shorthand for all that seasonal and cultural information. So when I make the leap from the kigo to the rest of the poem I can't help but be more engaged. Hopefully it shows in the poems.

JG: Impermanence is one of the characteristics of living we often find most discomforting. When we are enjoying ourselves, it is especially difficult to let go of the moment. However, we know it can't be otherwise and without it life would be static, no new experiences could arise, so we accept it willingly or not. I have so enjoyed this exchange of ideas and poems with you that I am very reluctant to end it. I am glad I had the chance to read your poems closely, to unveil their and your many virtues and artistry. I feel as if we took a long walk in the woods together, talking as we went along and stopping sometimes to look at something that struck us as interesting. Mainly, though, I am glad I had the chance to get to know you. You are a standard bearer of the values we cherish in humanity. I hope we have a chance again in the future to work together on other projects. And, thank you for giving of your time and thoughts and self, for your generosity.

pm: It was my pleasure, Jack. You've been a most kind host, and I'd be lying if I said I didn't gain from this as well. Michael Dylan Welch reminded me yesterday about a position I apparently held a year ago which I have softened a bit on. I doubt I'll ever reach a place where my convictions are fixed and I completely understand my poetics (wouldn't that be boring!), so exchanges like this give me lots to think about. And for that I thank you.

Artisan of the Imagination: An Interview with Peter Yovu

JG: Hello, Peter. Welcome to A Hundred Gourds.

PY: Hello, Jack. Thanks for inviting me here.

JG: First, I'd like to congratulate you on your most recent book, Sunrise (Redmoon Press, 2010). I intend to ask you questions from works in the collection, but feel free to roam wherever your mind takes you.

PY: Fair enough.

JG: Peter, I am especially drawn to one of the poems in the collection, because it works by lack of grammar, in this case punctuation. The poem is the following:

> where am I here

I find at least two meanings in the poem. The first is obviously where am I as a question and here as the answer, but without the question mark before here we are led to uncertainty and the whole line becomes a greater question: where am I here. The lack of grammatical marks thus creates a continuous uncertainty, which is what the poem is meant to be. It reminds me of Neitzsche's famous line that we cannot get rid of God because we still believe in grammar. How I understand Neitzsche here is that grammar is the way we structure and understand the world and ourselves as an order, a design, and so we postulate and create what we take as a given rather than a choice. Also, your poem evokes all those biblical passages where God asks a patriarch or prophet where are you and the quizzical answer is always "I am here," as if that were sufficient explanation. But, we live in a different episteme and "here" no longer suffices as an answer to where we are.

Given the profundity of the question raised by writing a poem whose meaning is based on its lack of grammar, I wonder why you did not probe this question in more poems in the collection.

You do have another poem that creates utter uncertainty in the face of great emotional loss by utilizing loss of our lexicon to express this

> word of his death
> bees streaming out of a hole
> in the dictionary

but this poem retains a grammatical structure, nonetheless (as the lack of punctuation after the first line is a haiku convention and does not add to the meaning of the poem).

PY: Jack, first off I should say that my response to this and other questions is not likely to follow strict logic, or even unstrict logic. I tend to think by association and by looking at things indirectly, a manner born perhaps from being somewhat shy, I try to make direct eye contact, but sometimes I land on a nose or chin and go with what I find there.

When I put the book together, my belief was that by looking at pretty much everything I'd written (and published) over the previous ten years or so, I would discover themes, threads, obsessions, connections and so forth, that I was largely unconscious of over that time. (Even if someone writes from an objective viewpoint, I think there are still likely to be unconscious impulses which lead one to write about certain things and to choose subject matter even when it may appear to simply present itself intentionally).

Odd as it may seem, your question actually helps me understand the placement of this poem in the book. I'll think out loud a little. The first section of the book has something to do with innocence, mostly, and unselfconsciousness which nonetheless begins to erode. Let me say in the state of innocence (pediatrician Donald Winnicott referred to childhood as going on being, there is only a sense of being here, or here-ness.   When Adam and Eve were expelled from Eden they were no longer here but in some form of perpetual there. Surely it can be said of most of us that we are seldom here but mostly believe that here, the place where we can be fulfilled, is somewhere else, over there? Searching, searching.

> where am I here

seems to relate to the condition of expulsion, and of searching. It makes sense, sense I can now attach to it because of your question, Jack, that such a place would lack structure, lack ground-- in other words, be without grammar, and yes, without certainty. It opens up a sense of falling, and that is a theme explored throughout the book. Falling, and holes.

The more I look at it, the more I feel the pain of this four syllable poem. It is possible that this may be one reason I did not explore the question that has arisen for you (and now me) around how a poem without clear grammatical structure may nonetheless (or all the more) have meaning.

The pain is inherent in the uncertainty, the groundlessness of how the poem works and in the acute self-consciousness it embodies. In fact, it barely embodies at all, and that is part of the pain. The body can only be here, which is why many meditation and mindfulness practices focus on it.

But this poem seems to have lost a body, and the poems that follow, while not as lost, in different ways speak to that condition. I believe Antoine de Ste. Exupery has written about his experience when, piloting his small plane, he temporarily lost all sense of horizon (both outside and on his instrument panel, I believe) and did not know, utterly, which way was up, which way was down. He was here, but where was he here?

A moment of terror.

So for me, it's a good question, one that speaks to my wishing to understand myself as a poetical/spiritual/psychological being. Does a poet need to examine the ways the structure of language may limit, or predetermine poetic expression? Of course, but I think depending on the inner strength of the writer, this examination could open new possibilities of perception, or it could lead to great disorientation. I do tend to believe that an artist or spiritual explorer needs to risk disorientation.

        where am I here

is kind of locked up in itself. It's a traffic jam on a roundabout.
"Word of his death," though also a poem of pain and loss, nonetheless seems to embody the possibility of movement and change. For the Sufis, bees have great significance, perhaps because they represent the beings that make sweetness in the hive of the heart. Many meanings can be derived from the poem, but one sense could be that the spirit at some point needs to move on to a new workplace; it has outlived the old one with its worn out tools and overused blueprints. There is joy inherent in the poem because it has a heart, at least an implied one.

JG: Let's move to another subject, Peter, one that bears on meaning, relates to grammar, and is one of the key elements in poetry. I am, of course, referring to lineation. I know that you do not consider yourself a haiku poet per se, but a poet influenced by haiku, who writes haiku-influenced, haiku-informed verse. As such, you do not adhere to conventional strictures, such as writing in three lines, necessarily, with a 5-7-5 sound unit to each line respectively. Once, however, we release ourselves from technical strictures, the line in verse becomes problematical. After all, poetry is not prose broken into shorter lines to look like poetry. I have in mind looking at two of your verses that use what I would suggest are unusual patterns and then set them side by side with some that are more conventionally structured, so that perhaps we can conclude something about lineation in verse in general.
The first poem is a good example of how ending a line with a preposition works, whereas usually this would be frowned upon as being somewhat shapeless:

        coming out of
          a hard house
            the flowering dawn

I think this choice of lineation works for two reasons. The first is mimetic. Dawn is not sudden, but gradual, seeping slowly over things until it reaches a certain height in the sky. Secondly, I think it is a matter of the breath that dictates the lineation. If the preposition "of" were put at the start of the second line, the reader would suffocate from the restriction of the form.
Here is another poem that utilizes an unusual lineation:

                    peels scattered throughout
                         the grove: Osiris' es-
                            sence drips from my mouth

I have two views of this poem and why you chose to enjamb, break the word
"essence" and place it in two lines. This is a striking example of dexterity in
lineation considering that essence is what is intrinsic, what cannot by definition be
broken down further in the nature of something. The first, and more likely, is that
Osiris, being the god of sprouting vegetation and fertility, is the superabundance of
new life, spring, and this is well-ensconced in your vigorous language, "dripping,"
"scattered." In short, Osiris's essence cannot be contained it is so prolific and hence
the enjambment, the splicing of the word to concretize this. My second view of the
poem is based on the fact that as written it falls into syllables of 5-7-5; so, it is
possible that you are being ironic in breaking "essence," which cannot be broken, to
demonstrate to what lengths it may be necessary to write in the traditional haiku
mode.
In either event, I would like to now place alongside these two above poems a few
poems that I find more conventionally lineated, to see if a different affect and tone
is achieved. What I have in mind are poems that don't end in prepositions or
transitive verbs or conjunctions, but are tighter knit.
Here are a few examples:

                    I know something's there
                         in the dark
                           in my body

                    a star
                    millions of wings trembling
                    in a cave

                    under a budding maple
                    all that I am
                    unable to say

Without referring to content or interpretation, although it may be impossible to
avoid, I find the latter poems to be more somber in tone, to be deeper and rich in the
sound they make and the meaning they evoke. It is not that they are superior
poems, it's just that because their form in no way calls attention to itself the reader
can forget form and the result is the content is perhaps more constant. If I were
drawing on metaphor, I would say the latter three poems sound like they are played
on a classical instrument, whereas the above two more experimentally lineated
poems sound as if played on electronic instruments. Having said this, I wonder if
you'd mind sharing with us what determinates go into your choices as to how to
lineate your verses.

37

PY: Jack, for me first and foremost is that I write something in a manner which I hope will indicate how I wish it to be read, preferably out loud.

Even such short poems as these have a body-- to read them (though perhaps not all of them) out loud is to partake of their embodiment. I think I may have said this elsewhere, but it is my belief that while a poem will evoke different thoughts, associations, and reveries for different readers through how it is taken to mean, the bodily experience of reading-- how its consonants makes the mouth move, how the vowels resonate in the head, throat, chest and belly, will be more or less basic and similar for all. This is why singing together can be such a profound experience-- bodies in communion. No doubt prayer as well. Also my belief that the body has its own form of knowing which is more essential than how the mind knows. This probably relates to the subconscious. From this point of view there is something in us, something wrapped in pure feeling, which longs to emerge, to come into the light of expression. To know itself. Interaction with the world via the senses is one way, perhaps the only way for this to happen-- for us to know ourselves, but from a somewhat mystical standpoint, it may also be true that the world knows itself through us. Doesn't Rilke talk about this?

So I may have gone off track a bit here, but I did warn you about that. I'm an off-track thinker, not by choice, but by discovery: to take myself by surprise, before I have a chance to compose myself or compose the world. This means, really, to find myself saying what wants to be said not what I think should be said. And maybe that's how the lineation of the poems works (when they work)-- as a kind of discourse between body and mind where the body holds sway, even though it has invited the mind to come into play. What I seem to be saying is the body, primordial feeling, wants the mind to shed some light on it, but does not want to be overwhelmed or replaced by the mind.

Here is another angle on this, and I take it from Iain MacGilchrist's wonderful book The Master and His Emissary, which is an examination of Western Civilization through the lens of the study of the brain hemispheres. He says that the right hemisphere is primary; its orientation is toward wholeness, to the totality of what is present and presented. The left hemisphere's orientation is more analytical-- it takes what has been presented to it apart in order to see how it works. It makes a representation of reality, and has a tendency to believe that representations are more real than the more holistic, intuited, implicit reality of the right hemisphere. Nonetheless, when both hemispheres are in a healthy relationship with each other, the left hemisphere's view will be reabsorbed, so to speak, by the right hemisphere and enlarged there. I don't want to see this in too concrete a manner (which would be the left hemisphere way) but to use it as a way of talking about how something inchoate in us wants to roll around in the light awhile and bring what it has learned back into the fold, so the darkness may shine.

To look more specifically at the poems you present: I like what you say about coming out of- if I were reading this or any of the poems out loud I would honor the line breaks-- a palpable pause on the word of.

But I also like reading a poem (out loud) several times with slightly different emphases-- shorter or longer pauses, or maybe hanging out with certain sounds, like letting the vibration of of spread out and find some kind of resolution or amplification in the softer f of flowering?

This is all based really on the enjoyment of the body. It's a very sensual approach (to what may often seem mental poems). I think reading one line poems is another matter, and maybe we'll touch on this later.

About peels scattered throughout? yes, this is a poem that, to follow what I said before, the analytical mind becomes engaged with rather quickly in trying to get at why essence is broken as es/sence. Is it merely put on the Procrustean bed of haiku's traditional 5/7/5 structure? Does it mimic Osiris' dismemberment, or the dripping from the mouth? I think if a poem leaves a reader too strongly with the question why, and does not resolve, almost simultaneously, in a heartfelt way of course, then it probably fails. Certainly there can be a tension between the two, which may lead back to the quality of uncertainty discussed earlier. It will be up to readers to determine if this works in this particular poem.

However, the questions that arise from reading the poem on the page may not arise from hearing it read out loud, where the mimetic quality of dripping would be evident, as least as emphasized by me. So maybe it's possible to say that the experience of the poem as spoken is very different from that of the experience of reading on the page. To be more direct about it, the lineation is determined by the action of breath and body. I do enjoy the play of analysis which happens on the page and in the mind, however. Having said this, I feel I need to look at poems I've written which give primacy to thinking and do not come to fullness (embodied, implicit feeling) when read out loud. There may be more than I think, and if I were writing a review of the book I would probably get into this.

Yes, and though I stay away from calling myself a haiku poet, I will admit that there is something in me that is attracted to the 5/7/5 blueprint and likes to play off and with it. Maybe it's like agreeing to have four limbs (I'm a quadropus) and not the eight of an octopus. The body has limits which the dance, for one, plays off and with. There is no exceeding (and maybe no excelling) without limits. Seeds and cells.

I find what you say about the more traditionally lineated poems very interesting and instructive, that they have a more somber tone. It raises questions that I do not have ready answers for, but which may relate to the nature of grief. Would it be true to say that grief does not need a strong exposure to the mind in order to be expressed? In other words, it is not a matter of play and of examination. With grief and deep sadness, the bones themselves speak.

And yet. . .

I like your metaphor of classical/electronic instruments. I enjoy some electronic music-- some things by Aphex Twin, or Pete Namlook for example, or Michael Brook with his infinite guitar. But it does seem to go straight to the head-- it can lack warmth, and ironically, I think a number of composers of electronic music go to great lengths to achieve a quality of sound inherent in real instruments. Analogue rather than digital. But one can arrive at effects and sounds via synthesizers which are not possible by other means. As this relates to poetry, I would say that experimentation-- including with lineation (which is akin to choreography)-- can yield interesting and important results but if it does not touch something in us, it may not go beyond interest and analysis. So my question is this: are there feelings and experiences in the core of our being-- including depths of grief-- which can only be revealed by exploration and experimentation? I feel (and think) the answer is yes.

JG: Peter, let's turn our attention to another related matter, and that is how many lines you set your poems in. The convention of three line poems has its origins in the three parts of the Japanese haiku, which in turn relate to the number of sound units in each part (5-7-5 sound units each bearing a distinct name in Japanese). Once, we vacated the traditional usage decades ago, the three line poem was more vestigial than anything else. Of course, the three line poem does still have its advantages: it is useful for narrative or dramatic poems as it provides a format for beginning, middle, and end.

Let's take a look at some of your poems and see how you use the number of lines they're written in to most advantage.
Here is an excellent example of one of your one-line poems:

>   snow I know everywhere to touch you

My first impression is that this is a concrete poem, as the elements in it are presumably all supine: the snow, the lovers; so it is natural that the poem should be written flat, in one line. Then, as a matter of formatting, the metonymy between snow and the prone lovers is strengthened in the placement you have them in. Additionally, it seems to me that the nakedness, the clarity of snow equates to the nudity and transparency of the beloved: both are completely revealed and having them set off in such proximity emphasizes this fact. Finally, the length of time on a snowy day for the lover to learn everywhere to touch the beloved is elongated by the one line.
Now, let's have a look at a two line poem, a form rarely used in haiku-like, haiku-informed poems:

>   the galactic aquarium shatters
>   our arms ending in starfish

I think the two line format for this poem is especially well-chosen, as the subject of the poem is the I and not-I, and the way to the participation mystique between all things. It is a poem about duality, but a questionable duality. What separates us from being aware of the oneness of things, so that our hands are the starfish in the cosmical sea, is a transparent membrane, like the glass in an aquarium, or what we call the self or ego; it is there but really lacks substance, permanency. Once we recognize that we are what we are conscious of; once we realize our nature is the Greater Nature, the galactic aquarium, the membrane, the glass shatters and we enter what anthropology once called the participation mystique, the mystical awareness of the unity of things.

Now, let's have a look at a three line poem from your collection. I'm choosing one that is unique, inasmuch as it relies on duplication of sounds, is somewhat onomatopoeic, as this satisfies the criteria of a three line poem and will also foreshadow my next question to you.

> mosquito she too
> insisting she
> is is is is is

The poems is wonderfully mimetic as it perfectly conveys the nature of the subject, the persistence of mosquitos, how once they have you in their sights they keep returning to you, no matter how often you try to brush them away, and the irritating sound to us of their continuous buzzing by us is delightfully onomatopoeic. The three line format allows you to incrementally introduce the features of the subject and this is one of its greatest strengths.

Now, having looked at some of the ways you format your poems, would you mind sharing with us what decisions you make in concluding the number of lines you compose an individual poem in.

PY: Lineation for me is pretty much determined by how I would like a poem to be read by others. That's a general principle for me, but one I don't necessarily stick to, and at times other principles take over, as when I wish a given line, usually the last, to come as a surprise or to play with expectation. I believe our senses are most alive when what we believe to be the case turns out not to be the case. An example might be looking at a tree just after snowfall, and seeing a penetrating blue between branches and assuming it is the sky when in actuality it is that blue that pockets of snow can fill with. There is a moment between assumption and knowledge which is very alive, when the sensation is most pure. I can't help mentioning the famous dictum of Basho about "going to the pine to learn from the pine"-- I think it may be more accurate to say "go to the pine but look a little away from it; take it in with your peripheral vision, as if by accident". Peripheral vision and hearing allows surprise. Dickinson of course said, "Tell all the truth but tell it slant".

So setting up expectation and then upsetting it is something a three line poem can do which a one line poem cannot. There's manipulation to it, but I doubt it will be effective or authentic unless the sense of surprise inheres for the author as well. So even there, the lineation is directing the reader, especially if the line break is honored with a brief pause, even where there is enjambment.

A single line poem operates differently for me. From what I've read numerous times, there seems to be a belief, at least among some readers and writers of haiku, that the single line poem is "appropriate" when dealing with-- with what?-- horizontal events or structures, let's say, like trains or the horizon or something. So Jack, you have read

snow I know everywhere to touch you

somewhat in this manner, but have given it a dimensionality I appreciate. It is entirely possible that I was impelled to go with one line for reasons you've given. However, for me, the one line poem can, at times, operate as a kind of proto-poem, presenting raw data (psychic data; sense data, etc.) without exactly sorting it out, and leaving it for the reader to do so, perhaps even more than is typical of haiku. The reader must determine the speed of reading, must determine emphasis and other elements. The reader may be invited to find alternative ways of reading such a poem, may find parallels, or contradictions or confusions between the discovered versions.

I don't think one line poems come from some kind of wish to innovate. For myself, through the inspiration of haiku having been lead to explore the nexus of poetry and perception, (let's say raw, or wild, perception), it seems a natural or organic development. My interest in this nexus predates my interest in haiku, and probably lead me to it, as to a quantum stepping stone.

So I am interested in the all-at-onceness of perception, the layers and co-occurrences. Haiku speaks to this, of course, and enacts it, by juxtaposing images. Everything is juxtaposed, from boson to bison to binary stars. And probably, not to get too mystical about this, it's a whole lot more intimate than juxtaposition, unless one believes that this is a world of one separate thing next to another separate thing.

So for me, and I hadn't thought about this until now, juxtaposition is a rather misleading term. It's technically, and superficially correct, but that's about it. So with a really good haiku (true of poetry and art in general) there can be two responses: one which notices and even admire technique-- "she's very skillful at juxtaposing surprising images"; and, another which comes from a discovery similar to that of the author, that two or more things arise from a single field simultaneously, in some sort of harmony, even if it may be perceived as discordant or disturbing.

It's just saying really that art transcends, but is not separate from technique. A pine tree is bound to the technique of its DNA, and perhaps in the laboratory would be mainly admired for that, but under the stars, in the context of everything, it is everything. Ken Wilber has offered a concept which I find useful. He recognized that particles, for example, are whole things unto themselves. Electrons, neutrons, etc., are whole things unto themselves. An atom is another whole thing unto itself, comprised of those smaller things-- it has all their attributes and something more. A molecule takes this a step further-- it has all the attributes of atoms and the particles which comprise them, but has something more, something they don't. And so on. He uses the term holon to describe this sense of particles being somehow complete.

In more human terms, you could say that a child is only a child, (and a good thing too), but an adult has all the attributes of a child within the larger field of maturity. So art transcends but is rooted in technique. Actually, I'm not comfortable with that, because it gives technique a primacy I don't believe it has. I go back to what I said earlier-- technique is in the service of insight and discovery. The unconscious calls the conscious mind down to help give shape to something which wants to be understood.

To get back: for me the impulse of the single line poem, at least in some instances, comes from the understanding of co-occurrence, and pushes the technique of juxtaposition a little further, further and at the same time back to something more primitive (prime-ative; first-ative), where in the best sense, things are still confused. I would also say that art transcends intention. What intention can there be, in artistic or spiritual practice, other than to be open to what needs to be born? I find that there is a good possibility with one line poems that something will emerge which not only transcends intention, but may reveal something difficult or disquieting. (Equally it may reveal the opposite). If an author says, no, I don't like that particular nuance or interpretation, and works to eliminate it, something is likely to be lost. The truth may be lost, its impulse to be seen thwarted.

A poem which maybe speaks to this possibility is

uneasy things grow wings underground

but a poem which enacts it more may be this one:

sunrise darkens the face I dream with

which implies things I don't particularly like, though I don't truly know why, even while it implies things that impel me. Maybe for this reason I ended up feeling it was the most authentic poem in the book, and why I honored it by calling the book Sunrise.

JG: As promised, Peter, my last question technically to you concerns something akin to onomatopoeia in poetry. The question harkens back to a discussion you began on your blog Sails at The Haiku Foundation in the summer of 2011 and which I feel was never satisfactorily completed. If you recall, you suggested that there was a more originary language than our current language that was more wild, that relied more heavily on sound, that, in fact, meaning adhered essentially to sound in it as opposed to the sound/meaning divide in current languages (although thinking about it it could just as well apply to a new language, as well). You were discussing an article in a similar vein written by Martin Lucas and included in Evolution (Redmoon Press, 2010) and you extrapolated the following from it: you were saying that poetry had an irrational element to it that was lost in interpretation or paraphrase and you went on to conjecture regarding this irrationality that "this quality is inherent in a poem and explication (which cannot present something but can only represent something) drives it away. This means, essentially, that Poetic Spell (the body of the poem) indeed does not operate at the level of linguistic meaning, but closer to the way music operates, affecting us, but "not with meaning per se." It is "how a poem is experienced or felt before being taken up by the conscious mind."

Now, in Sunrise, you provide an example of what you mean by such a poem in one you wrote and included in the volume:

> millionating beast
> quadramillion hooves
> drum down the groundskin

It's a marvelously inventive poem, in which you create words and rely on sound to create meaning: the ever-multiplying magnitude of the power of the thundering sound of being and creation.

My question to you is wherein lies the importance to you of poetry relying essentially on its sound and thus being somewhat dissociated from its meaning, or put otherwise, that meaning would adhere in language's sound alone, without reference to its signified or referred meaning. As I know from my own practice of writing, the sound of words sometimes does not convey the emotion I wish and then I'm sometimes forced to write off-subject to convey the emotion a particular confluence of things evoked. This stems from the fact that there is no natural relationship between words and things and I think you would like to have a "natural" language where such a relationship exists.

PY: It's a big question. I doubt if it can or really should be completely addressed, or that any exploration will satisfy, unless it is to the extent that exploration itself has a quality of satisfaction to it-- the satisfaction of uncertainty? I think that's the nature of poetry, to enable us to reside a while in uncertainty. I don't know if that's the same thing as Frost's "a temporary stay against confusion", but it may be an element of it.

My sense is that within the language we use everyday, or misuse every day, there exists something which is already originary, as you put it, and which we respond to on the level of the body. I don't think my thoughts about this are at all new. Discussing it, I get caught in a dilemma I often feel when writing about what some people call haiku. So maybe I can digress a bit here and say a few things about that. I am uncomfortable saying that what I write is haiku. Sometimes that feels like a cop-out to me, but I find it helpful-- I don't have anyone's chin on my shoulder whispering Japanese words I don't understand in my ear. My discovery of haiku many years ago opened up for me the possibility that with just a few words one could be in the presence of great power, poignancy, mystery, otherworldliness, clarity, precision, space, present-moment nostalgia and so on. I cannot say what it is, but I feel there is an impulse underlying Japanese haiku which opened up those discoveries for people like Basho, but which cannot be bound to Japanese culture. The impulse resided and still resides in a chamber of the human psyche, universally. Can it be otherwise? I do not even know that the Japanese were the first to open that chamber, but they certainly helped reveal it to the world. An analogy would be African-Americans opening up the jazz/blues chamber of the psyche for exploration by cultures around the world. It's a mystery how this happens, how discoveries are made and unlit bulbs on the switchboard light up around the world.

So for me, I like to think that I can be in touch with that impulse, and to let it go where it wants. The impulse needs nutrition, of course, which comes from reading and discussing, but I don't think it wants to stop there, from it has learned. It wants to throw out all kinds of things, just to see if they work. Kind of like nature's profligacy-- all those beetles.

That wanting is going to take me away from any concentration I may have on what I or anyone else believes is haiku, though as I've said before, I want to give the believers a lot of encouragement and gratitude and a slice of pizza if necessary, because they are going in the direction they must and maybe after years of diligent practice will show up with a beetle I will cherish. Which leads me to say, though, that too many haiku have pins through their backs-- are specimens in a case. But we all know that any really good, living, wild poem is rare.

So how does this apply to sound? I guess it does insofar as what I say may have more relevance to the freedom and play in the kind of writing that interests me than in "haiku". It may be more relevant to questions around what capacities very short verbal utterances can have. So much is made, in discussions about haiku, about the image, and the juxtaposition or disjux between two images. This is a marvelous thing, to put two images together and to see what happens. I think I've said already, that even if one is taken by an image from the outside, it is somehow prompted from the inside. Something inside says "you need to look at that". Or something happens, a toad's throat billows and there is a bracket fungus on a nearby tree that looks like a toad's throat. Many times one might notice something like that and not take it in, until that inner impulse arises and says, "no, take this in". So where images come from, why they come and how, is pretty mysterious.

But it may be true that there are sounds in the body, let's stick with vowel sounds that are quietly humming to themselves, minding their own business when something shows up and they get a bit excited and want to enter the picture so to speak. The heart is quietly going "ahh" and the mind going "eee" by day and "ooo" in sleep and the belly is going "ohhhh" and then something stirs the heart or the mind or the belly or all three and they want to come up out of the throat and be heard, they want the toad and the fungus to know they are loved, or maybe feared or maybe both . . .

45

Then the vowels realize they need the modifying aspects that the consonants bring. The vowels are the spirit-sounds and the consonants are the body sounds that help shape them, bend them, give them something to hold onto and let go of. So all this is happening-- it least that's what I'm proposing-- below the level of consciousness, or of conscious meaning. They just want to get in the picture, to be the soundtrack. We're watching the movie, we get what the images mean, the symbols and so on, but we feel the music. There's nothing very original in what I'm saying.

So the sound of words is another layer of juxtaposition. It is calling back down to those places of origin in the body, where more vowel sounds are just forming and responding and we feel our heart open (or hurt), we feel our mind cleaned out by the higher pitches, we feel our belly soften, of stiffen, or. . . . And none of this is yet speaking to rhythm and beat and how that affects the muscles and the bones. Others have written about this very well, and probably more practically than I am here. Donald Hall, for example, in his essay "Goatfoot, Milktongue, Twinbird". I think I have that right. Or Robert Frost, when he refers to sound as "the gold in the ore". He continues: "Then we will have the sound out alone and dispense with the inessential. We do till we make the discovery that the object in writing poetry is to make all poems sound as different as possible from each other, and the resources for that of vowels, consonants, punctuation, syntax, words, sentences, meter are not enough. We need the help of context--meaning--subject matter. That is the greatest help toward variety". To me this is saying what I'm trying to say from another angle. In one sense he is saying that the world is calling out to sound, saying "if you deal with me you will make a different sound than ever before". I am suggesting that sound itself guides experience. So we can juxtapose these to two directions and perhaps find perfect overlap. I believe I said elsewhere that different poets may favor one "direction" over another. I think many a lot of poets who write for Roadrunner are exploring the "sound guiding experience" direction, and also the "image guiding experience" and "language guiding experience" directions.

Looked at from the metaphor of brain hemispheres, the left side of the brain only wants meaning-- it wants everything in the laboratory lined up and examinable. Laboratories are very quiet places really. The scientist may be content to hang out right there, with meanings pinned to the table and explicit, but the poet, who may also want meaning and subject matter, is available to the call of the right hemisphere and opens the doors to sound, the vowels, consonants etc. coming out to embrace the specimens and wrap them in implicit love, trailing clouds of the sweet night they have come from.

So maybe what I am saying is that sound is the element of the poem that gives meaning meaning-- felt meaning; implied meaning. I think of how big some trees are at night-- enormous-- and how that changes by the light of day. And how in either case a little breeze wraps them in otherworldliness.

And these matters are clearly important for poets in general, though LANGUAGE poets might think it all rubbish. My question is-- how does it apply to haiku, or to very short poems that have been injected with haiku-juice? I believe it does apply, but each will have to find out in what way. I have no good answer.

JG: Peter, we're running out of space and time, so I'd like to take this opportunity to express my gratitude to you for sitting through this interview. I consider you one of the few best haiku-influenced poets of our time and so it was a considerable delight to have shared your work and time with you. I also consider you one of our foremost thinkers and so it was with great anticipation that I awaited each of your answers to my questions. I mentioned above that the previous question was technically the last I'd put to you. The reason I put it that way is because I'd like to add one last poem to our dialogue, a self-portrait, as it were, and if you care to comment on it, now is the time.

> a shakuhachi flute
> I step into the wind
> with holes in my bones

Whether those holes you mention came from the many wounds you've accumulated in a lifetime, or whether they were openings you cultivated, we can't help but feel that it is precisely because of them that when the world passes through you you make such hauntingly beautiful music.

> an unseen bird sings
> the dew is red is green is
> blue

PY: I take you to have some things in common with me, Jack, such as a great sensitivity which is open to the creative, but also to feeling things deeply, including hurt. I really like your poem: Real enough to feel a paper rose ("Notes from the Gean," 3:3) - maybe that speaks a bit to what I'm saying. Okay Jack.

JG: Okay, Peter. Thank you for sharing your time, your thoughts, your knowledge, and yourself with us. You've been very generous.

THE SUPERLATIVE QUOTIDIAN

The Superlative Quotidian: An Interview with Chris Gordon

JG: Hello, Chris. Welcome to A Hundred Gourds.

CG: Hello, Jack. Thank you for having me.

JG: I understand from reading some biographical material about you that you work with the developmentally disabled. Do you think this kind of work, exposing you to those who hold vastly different views of reality from those the majority consensus do, has influenced your poetry?

CG: Absolutely. I work with people who have altered brains. That's really the only definition. They need a little more support. Most of us get that naturally. We weren't separated from our families. Put into institutions. About a third of us will get a brain injury as an adult. It makes you see things differently. That's the first criteria for a poet.

JG: Well, I have to admit that in the past my own work brought me into institutions of the developmentally disabled and the rooms were caged and some of the people wore helmets to protect them from hurting themselves and I felt threatened emotionally and mentally. I take it for you such a population are now just a part of the human landscape and this widens your view of what's real and not real. Would that be fair to say?

CG: That was the 80s here in Oregon. The whole thing got toppled and it took about ten years to get people living and participating in the community. Most studies show that if we take care of the most vulnerable members of society, everyone receives better care at all stages of their life.

JG: Yes, I was referring to my experience at about the same historical period. I'm glad to hear things have changed and those with differing understandings of the "real" are included in the society at large. That explains to me in some small measure some of the series of poems you have been writing in the last three years, the three series of poems, Invisible Circus, Chinese Astronauts, and the Crow poems. They are all series of poems of the "unusual" squarely located in the most quotidian of environments and how they interact. Do you see any correlation?

CG: Absolutely. For me the quotidian has to be unusual, otherwise we've slipped into a kind of death. If we don't remake the world everyday, we've stopped paying attention and the animal within us has given up.

JG: Of the three series of poems I mention above, what was the chronological order you wrote them in?

CG: I wrote the Invisible Circus back in 2009 specifically for the first issue of MASKS. Bruno Munari's beautiful "Circus in the Mist" is one of my enduring favorites from my childhood and I took the English title as a leaping off point (the Italian title means something like "A Mist over Milano"). I decided I liked the idea of an Invisible Circus, calling to mind the Invisible Colleges of certain esoteric traditions. From there my fondness for Ray Bradbury took over and the sequence wrote itself. The whispers in Italian lead me to Il Corvo.

I wrote The Chinese Astronauts the following year. Despite its obvious affinity to the repeated image sequences that have proliferated recently, this isn't meant to be a metaphorical or potentially surreal poem. It's a paean to the actual three astronauts of Divine Craft 7 who were all born the same year as me. Not a very experimental entry into a poem, but I liked some of the surprises it yielded.

The crow sequence all came to me on a Saturday morning this past April. I was feeling a pressure to speak without the time or the venue to do so. They're still a little rough to me. Some distracting repetition and a lack of rhythm in some of them. I was also missing the single line form, which I used fairly exclusively up until 2006 when I started playing around more with the three line form. I felt that some of my single line haiku had become unwieldy, pushed to the 17 syllable limit and squandering the potential grace and slightness of the single line form.

JG: Before I begin discussing the individual works, I'd like to offer a general theory I have regarding them. It seems to me that you juxtapose, or create dysjunction to use a more modern term, what I call the supernal, or totemic, or extraordinary within the confines of the most commonplace and thereby create tension, confusion, pathos, profundity, the whole range really of human experience. That is why I asked you earlier about your work, because "madness" was long ago associated with possession by the divine and oracles and shamans and poets were considered touched by the divine. The title of your Chinese Astronauts, which was not included in Roadrunner Haiku Journal where it was published, was "Divine Craft," so I think I am on the right track.

So, let's take a look at "The Invisible Circus." For me it's one step beyond what we in childhood called the flea circus, but far steeper. It is hilarious, but also horrific in its way and I would like to know if you would agree that it is somewhat synonymous with the Unconscious, what goes on hidden behind the screen projection of the rational mind and world? As an example, let's take one poem first:

Your watch stopped when

You bought your ticket to

The Invisible Circus

Like the unconscious, particularly the id function, is timeless in psychoanalysis and is essentially without a negative (as that is part of the conscious mind). Do you agree with this understanding of the poem?

CG: Caveat emptor: Don't go to the Invisible Circus!

JG: Okay, Chris, we've been fairly warned and you have no liability should anything untoward befall us. Let me site a few more of the poems from Invisible Circus that lead me to interpret it as the unconscious.

Underneath the pillow

Making your neck ache

The Invisible Circus

This strikes me as tellingly pointing to the fact that access to the Invisible Circus is through dreams, precisely as psychoanalysis understands it.

The Invisible Circus

Goes from town to town

Never really moves

And, like the unconscious, though it is experienced in real time and space, it has no location other than the mind of the dreamer or person awake and aware of their unconscious thoughts.

Cut your thumbs on

The Bearded Lady

at The Invisible Circus

The knife at your throat

A hand down your pants

The Invisible Circus

These poems evoke the sexual ambivalence and sexual danger associated with unconscious desires, forbidden desires. Yet, desire is the capitol of the unconscious, isn't it?

The girls are all Clean

and well-oiled at

The Invisible Circus

CG: While I've been very conscious over the years of using such poetic tools as juxtaposition, indeterminacy, sampling, and randomness, to create haiku, I've been thinking in terms of images, feelings, senses, and the matter of the poem. That the difference lay in the comparison of elements, not so much in the valence of meaning or the shifting of themes or focus.

In other words, I haven't thought of it as an overlay of two different worlds, only an overlay of experiences. The mystical world and the mundane world are the same to me. Or so I strive to make them so. Sometimes it's easy. Sometimes it takes a great knack. Which is to say I'm very pleased you see this in my work.

JG: Chris there is even more evidence in the Invisible Circus series to suggest its relationship to the unconscious, which Freud remarked was always experienced as the uncanny by consciousness. Just consider the poem

Your limp goes

Away on the grounds of

The Invisible Circus

or,

Everyone speaks Italian

in whispers at

The Invisible Circus

or,

The cards are all

Blank at the tables at

The Invisible Circus

All of these poems clearly are impossible to the rational mind, yet common enough and plausible enough if dreamt; the unconscious as the realm of the uncanny and fantastic seems evident to me in the above poems. How do you experience these poems? Are they for you, as they are for me, emblematic of the co-existence of another, spectacular and menacing (sacred) world behind the scenes while simultaneously within the scenes of everyday life? And wouldn't you agree that some of our deepest fears exist in this realm of dreams and suppressed thoughts in reality? Just look at this powerful, fairytale-like poem in the collection:

Your blind grandmother

Almost sold you to

The Invisible Circus

It awakens all our deepest dread of ambivalence towards those we most trust as children and it does so with some humor, given an invisible circus and a blind woman, one who could not see what is not even visible.

CG: Yes, the Invisible Circus could be synonymous with the unconscious. Yet at the same time the sequence is composed of very tangible elements, and while the poems may be impossible to the rational mind, they communicate perceptions and feelings that at their root are very rational, though perhaps uncomfortable and difficult to communicate.

Whatever the unconscious is, it's made of ideas. We live in a world of ideas. Some of these ideas are "real" and some of them are "insubstantial" or "fanciful." Somewhere in our minds and hearts all ideas have equal value and substance. This is where we dream. This is where we destroy ourselves. This is where we're reborn. This is where we tell stories. This is where we make sense of ourselves. This is where we make sense of the world.

JG: Chris, let's turn our attention to your second series, The Chinese Astronauts. This is a fascinating series that for me works on a similar principle to the Invisible Circus, except here, instead of an irruption of the uncanny and unconscious into the quotidian, we have the supernal, or divine, or extra-terrestrial in relation to the quotidian. The results, of course, alter the consequences significantly. And, in this series, you present both the pre-and-post orbit of the astronauts and this has great significance, as I see it. I think in the poems that address the preparation of the astronauts, we can see the ineptness (and its humor) of modern man to create a mythology of the modern age to live by. Then, in the post-orbit poems, where ordinary men have touched the divine, become extra-terrestrial (in the sense of having been freed of earth's atmosphere and gravity), I think we can see once again the inability of modern man to create a myth to live by, but the predominant feeling tone here is one of pathos. The Chinese, an atheist country, named the space-craft the Divine Craft and you followed suit in naming your series with the same title. The flight itself well represents what Joseph Campbell and Carl Jung, both interpreters of myth, the night sea journey, in which man goes on as symbolic voyage and is altered by the experience. However, to quote Campbell, modern man lacks this myth-making power in his modern incarnation. From Campbell (from Atheist Nexus):

"When you see the earth from the moon, you don't see any divisions there of nations or states. This might be the symbol, really, for the new mythology to come."

What is your experience of The Chinese Astronaut series and is it in keeping with the overview I have presented?

CG: No, there was no "night sea journey" for the Chinese Astronauts. They might as well have not gone into space. The only reason the astronauts are Chinese is because the poem's about some Chinese astronauts. If we took away the title of the poem and the reference to the Premier (in one of the poems you don't cite), they could be any astronauts.

Here's a poem I write a few years before the sequence:

The Astronaut

The Astronaut drove nine hundred miles in a diaper. They wear those sometimes for lift-off and re-entry. In the trunk of the car a steel mallet, rubber tubing, and some duct tape. Arriving at the airport at 3am she put on a wig and a trench coat and sprayed her romantic rival in the face with pepper spray. The other woman, who was apparently involved with the same Astronaut as the other Astronaut, managed to escape in her own car. The Astronaut's Lawyer said his client just wanted to have a talk with the woman. And sure. This makes sense. In space the most simple of tasks sometimes require a Herculean effort. This explains the diapers. This explains the rubber tubing. This explains the hacksaw. Maybe people shouldn't go into space. Maybe they should stay at home with their daughters and leave the steel mallet in the tool shed. Or maybe it's the other option. Places that are hard to get to. Maybe we should just stay there once we've arrived.

We are all astronauts. We are all shipwrecked on unfamiliar terrain with broken tools and unreliable habitats. Habits from the old days that frighten us and propel us forward. Make us ashamed before our ancestors.

The radio might work. But maybe no one's listening. In the mean time we'll use what we've got. Tell stories around the fire.

JG: If you don't mind, I'd like to visit the last poem, since it is my favorite and also shines light on the rift, at least for me, between the return of the astronauts to the ordinary world and their experience in space.

Back at their day jobs

The Chinese Astronauts

Remember weightlessness

This poem comes closest, I think, to fulfilling what Campbell had in mind as noted above. The colloquial expression of the first line sets the tone of the repetitive, heavy nature of the ordinary world and having passed through a transcendent experience, the astronauts do retain something: weightlessness or freedom. If we look at the pre-flight poems, I think we have a fine expression of the ineptitude, the inadequacy of man to create a mythos for this age.

Their hands fumble at

Pockets that aren't there

The Chinese Astronauts

The Chinese Astronauts

Aren't able to touch

Their own faces

The Chinese Astronauts

Their suits are different

Made in foreign countries

Their wives dress

Like stewardesses

The Chinese Astronauts

These poems read somewhat like slapstick spaceman works. Yet, they actually clearly express the dilemma of modern man: how to prepare for and create a legend equal to the modern world and signify this. We have an emphasis on awkwardness, on inabilities here. And, I think you create what I will call an idiomatic approach to underscore this fact. By idiomatic, I do not mean that you use idiomatic speech; what I have in mind is that the expressed scenes and actions are idiomatic in as much as there is a figurative meaning quite separate from the literal meanings depicted. Was this deliberate on your part?

CG: I would say no, as the literal meaning is an intentional distortion. I would say rather than the supernal entering the quotidian in these poems, we have the transcendent becoming the mundane. The Chinese astronauts are portrayed via banal tableaus or with incidental details of their journey, not exciting stellar vistas or important scientific tasks, not even noble efforts to better humankind. It's just another day at the job. The quotidian has not been infused with the vastness of the universe, this vastness has been reduced to a series of alienated tasks and photo opportunities.

JG: In the end, the Chinese Astronauts, have not gone through the night sea journey, have not gone through a mythic adventure and this is precisely the failure of modern man: he has no myths to live by. The first thing that strikes us is the economic interest of the astronauts; they have no apparent interest in opening the doors of perception, of psychic change and wholeness.

The payload's still

A mystery to

The Chinese Astronauts

Having gone through an extra-terrestrial experience, having "touched" the sublime, the government cannot represent this appropriately and here is one of what I earlier called idiomatic poems:

Carried from the capsule

The Chinese Astronauts

Sit in blue fold-out chairs

The best the government can do is create an ad hoc representation of space in the "blue...chairs." I feel a great pathos in this and the other post-space poems. What was once the great achievement of humankind, the power of mythmaking, is apparently lost and these poems highlight this fact to an unprecedented degree. How do you feel about this reading of the post-orbit Chinese Astronaut poems?

CG: If there is pathos here, my intention in that area is the portrayal of the degradation of the transcendent experience into the empty ritual.

Yes they had their moment with the divine, but it was temporary and passed. They were on everyone's minds for a week or two, and then they had to go back to their day jobs and feel an emptiness and longing for the rest of their lives.

We get to vicariously savor their pioneering efforts, without the damage of traveling to the limits of human experience. You can only touch the gods occasionally. Otherwise you die. It's like the pharmakon. The experiment. The messenger. That's the astronaut. They come back from a journey and are unable to translate that joy into their everyday life.

JG: Chris, let's finally turn to the last of the series you've written in the past three years, the Crow poems that you wrote in April 2011. I find them to be an intriguing reinvention of the archetype of the Trickster, a figure prominent in folklore, and an introduction of this figure within the world. The Trickster is often represented as an animal that plays tricks and otherwise disobeys the norms of culturally correct behavior. The Trickster, though it breaks the rules of the gods or nature, ultimately has a beneficial effect in the world. Let's take a look at some of the ways you express the amoral nature or mischievous nature of this figure.

a last few tricks ask the crow

a second glance at your wife the crow

cheats at love but not at cards the crow

implied by the crow numberless is the way to go

the crow gets you to pull down your pants

When you sat down to write on that day in April of 2011, did you conceive of a series of poems about this Native American archetype, or did you simply choose a subject and let your imagination go?

CG: My usual process is to start with an image or narrative fragment and see where it takes me. I don't typically write with themes or messages in mind. I find a compelling entry, sometimes, and develop it until I feel a sense of completion. So no, I wasn't thinking about the Trickster when I wrote the crow poems. But perhaps in some way I apparently was. I guess I'm just saying that my intention in writing is merely to create something that seems engaging to me afterwards rather than to muse upon an intended outcome.

JG: You know, I never found understanding the archetype of the Trickster easy until reading your poems. I can see now how the Crow, as a Trickster, transmutes the quotidian and thereby aids us in keeping alive, just what you alluded to earlier in the interview. The ordinary world seems made up of odd elements, and yet when put together, when fathomed, are a unity, even:

three plus five that's the crow

Or, the many facets of what the world is illustrated in this poem:

at the gem show he's invisible the crow

And, the Trickster also teaches us something about time, about what's important, about letting go, about the ordinary as both creator and creation:

never on time but never late the crow the crow has nothing to do with doors dances in the rain because he can the crow after you sleep the crow not really black he's purple the crow

Were all these functions of the Trickster archetype available to you consciously, or did some of them just spontaneously appear as you wrote the series?

CG: This is a piece of wisdom I got from William Stafford, a poet who has been very generous with his ideas about poetry and composition. His essay "A Way of Writing" (from Writing the Australian Crawl, University of Michigan Press, 1978) provided a new perspective for me that suddenly transformed much of my disregarded writing into my real poetry, so that my polished pieces seemed artificial and ungainly in comparison. I also found it easier to get my writing sessions started, having let go of the notion that I was trying to achieve an intended result.

In regards to the Trickster transmuting the quotidian, I found a brief series of haiku I wrote just prior to the Crow poems, which may explain the need for the emergence of a trickster. It's titled "The Dead Parts of Me." I've attached it. I would say they're the closest I've come to anti-haiku.

The Dead Parts of Me

onion grass my son pukes in the sink

nails one of them in my foot

the moon who cares where it is

your feet they're nicer than mine

bottle caps they rattle among the spoons

your panties entwined with my odd socks

the crow says something for the crows

asphaltheat and foreign policy

the dead parts of me pester the rest

stale crackers it's easy to put them back

the cat's meow what's that really about

the penny not as old as it looks

the extra napkin always gets tossed

raincheck nothing to do with the rain

your fingerprint consistent prostitute

the place on you I know you can't touch

box tops they usually tear anyway

sassafras people still actually say that

your twat I've never called it that

all the knives are clean I hit the lights

toothpaste not sure what I'm supposed to think

JG: In Native American Trickster myths, the Trickster, in this case Crow, allows us contact with the sacred through laughter and letting go of rigidly held categories of the real. I think this is a great triumph on your part, because certainly in this series of poems we are not dealing with two realms, but the sacred and secular are well joined. Crow takes us out of time, out of our usual understandings of the nature of the ordinary world, and leaves us in a newer version of the same world we already inhabited.

more than all you know the crow

did you say bless you to the crow

even in empty spaces the crow

your plans are funny to the crow

63

Do you think in this series, you have engaged in a modern myth making that is the prerogative of the poet and have succeeded in making the mundane and mystical one and the same?

CG: As for myth making, which can an intentional and mechanistic process, I would say I hope I'm just part of the process of receiving, remaking, and passing on the stories that have captivated me and encouraged me to be a poet in the first place

JG: Chris, I'm afraid we're running out of space and time, so I would like to make some remarks in closing. For those readers who would like to read your earlier work, they can find examples at your Blog/Publication Site ant ant ant ant ant haiku. I strongly suggest to readers that they take the time to read these works, because they answer a conflict that has arisen recently in the haiku community: whether haiku can be seen as equivalent to mainstream post-modernist art, on the one hand, or, on the other hand, whether mainstream post-modernist art lives up to the standards of what is traditionally construed as haiku. Chris Gordon answered this seeming dilemma seventeen years ago in the affirmative and continues to do so; his haiku is poetry of the highest order and complexity and remains true to the virtues of the tradition of the form. That he has been doing this alone for so long, without fanfare, steadfastly steering a new course for the genre says a great deal about his character and confidence and humility.

Chris has expressed to me that the three series we discussed represent the bulk of his haiku in the last three years, because he has turned his artistic talents and energies to the visual arts. For those interested, they can find an abundance of his art work at mrcr3w.deviant art. You will find beneath the examples a space bar to press which will reveal five pages of Chris's art. He is an accomplished artist working in photography, collage, and assemblages and if you take his hint about how he views his creative process, paying attention to the comparison of elements and overlaying of expressions, you will be richly rewarded. Even simply viewing the work will be sufficient, because they are so startlingly stunning that they will strike you on a visceral level.

Finally, I would like to say that Chris Gordon is a great teacher. He has shown me that by doing your best, you show self-respect as well as respect to others. This was something my father tried to teach me forty-five years ago and which I have only learned by working with Chris. So, I am grateful to him for reintroducing my father to me.

I believe that the three series of poems we reviewed in this interview represent his mature period: the poems are clean, clear, simple, with a lightness of touch, yet there is not the slightest sacrifice of profundity in them. This is much the same as it was for Matsuo Basho four centuries ago, when in his mature period he taught lightness as the essence of haiku.

CG:I just want to add in conclusion that I appreciate the high regard you have for my work, but I hope I'm not in my mature phase yet. I see the foundations of my work and their development, but I hope they continue to ripen and mature and change as long as I put thought and effort into them.

JG: Okay, Chris. It was been a pleasure and privilege to work with you.

CG: You're quite welcome, Jack. This has been an amazing process for me and I appreciate again all the time and thought you've put into my work.

Gathering Stones: An Interview with John Martone

JG: Hello, John. Welcome to Roadrunner Haiku Journal.

JM: Hi, Jack. Thanks for inviting me.

JG: John, from the title of your latest book, ksana (in Buddhist parlance the briefest moment of mental time or a temporal center) [published by Redmoon Press, 2009], to viewing your photographs of various Buddhas under the title "Supplement to the Saddharma Pundarika Sutra Chapter 1" at the journal "otoliths" (issue 22, 2011), it became obvious that you are a Buddhist. There was a time when I was a practicing Buddhist and also writing haiku. At that time, I felt a conflict existed between the two pursuits. Then, when I read in Awakening The Buddha Within (Broadway Books, 1997) by Lama Surya Das that Allen Ginsberg, who was entering a one-month retreat, brought pen and notebook to write haiku after meditation had them snatched away by Trungpa Rinpoche because the idea was to stop collecting transient thought bubbles, I felt confirmed that a conflict existed. Do you feel a conflict in pursuing these two paths, John?

JM: Vipassana meditation involves observing phenomena with bare attention, and letting them go, as Trungpa Rinpoche's taking Allen's notebook makes clear. One sees how everything is suffering, impermanent and not-self.

Is writing poems clinging to the illusion of self? A poem is a cry. Is a cry an illusion? Does an illusion cry out? What else ever could?

One wants language itself to do the speaking, linked as it is to the perceptual act. Strip away all the commentation, as Cid demanded, elaboration.

Above all, one doesn't want dramatic "set pieces" those "little dramas" as Brooks and Warren saw poetry in antediluvian days and as most everyone still does. And worse still, those personal essays masquerading as poetry and the 'poet as rock star' sensibility spawned by the mags.

There are very great Buddhist poets – poets who are Buddhists – Thich Nhat Hanh, Ko Un, Issa, Basho, Saigyo, Wang Wei, all the way back to the Therigatha and Theragatha – the poetry of the Pali canon, and the Buddha's own words – his fire sermon, snake, etc. Of course, one would be a fool to think that because they were able to...

John Ireland has a very good pamphlet about Vangisa – one of the poets of the Theragatha. Vangisa was said to have recited a poem in response to one of the Buddha's teachings. The Buddha asked if he had composed the poem spontaneously (first thought best thought!), and when Vangisa answered that he had, Buddha asked him to compose another. Once, when the Buddha spoke on the right speech, Vangisa responded with another poem – to the Buddha's approval. It must be one of the first poems about poetry. Here is a bit of it, in Ireland's prose:

Truth is indeed the undying word; this is an ancient verity. Upon truth, the good say, the goal and the teaching are founded.

The sure word of the Awakened One speaks for the attainment of nibbana, for making an end of suffering, is truly the best of words.

If the Vangisa story doesn't put the conflict to rest (and it didn't in medieval Japan), there's also Muju Ichien's Sand and Pebbles or Shasekishu, a wonderful book from 13th century that we have in Robert Morrell's translation. One of the book's themes is poetry as a way to realization. There's one passage that makes the point so concisely, that I'm surprised it's not mentioned all the time:

Now we refer to the poetry of "wild words and specious phrases" as "defiled poetry," because it lures us to attachment, imbues us with a vain sensuality, and decks us out with empty words. But poetry may express the principles of the Holy Teaching, accompany a sense of impermanence, weaken our worldly ties and profane thoughts and cause us to forget fame and profit. If, on seeing leaves scattered by the wind, we come to know the vanity of the world; and if, on composing a verse on the moon hidden in the clouds, we come aware of the unsullied Principle within our hearts, then poetry mediates our entry upon the path of Buddha and becomes a reliable tool for understanding the Law. Accordingly, men of old practiced the Law of Buddha without rejecting the Way of Poetry.

Despite such encouragement, I often suspect the best stop talking or feel no need to. It would take real courage to live a life of silence. A maternal aunt of mine, Sr. Ellenita, recently died at 92, after a lifetime in silence in the convent laundry room.

I am a pretty hopeless case. By and large, poets are.

JG: To follow up in a similar vein, in the Modern Haiku (Vol. 41.1) review of ksana, Marshall Hryciuk points out that the Redmoon Press version of your book is a compilation of some twenty hand- made chapbooks of your poems that you previously put together and distributed freely. Obviously, there's a politics involved in producing your own books and distributing them for free: it removes the poems from the marketplace as a commodity form and circumvents what Walter Benjamin discussed in his famous essay, "The Work of Art in the Age of Mechanical Reproduction," which was the alienation of the art from its producer-the artist. What was it that persuaded you to have your chapbooks published and distributed through Redmoon Press?

JM: Zukofsky said we write just one poem – and of course, Whitman added to Leaves of Grass over the years. I call that a lifepoem, and so from time to time I want to pull things together, as with ksana and dogwood & honeysuckle before it, and now with ocean. But perhaps I am rationalizing.

Giselle Maya is an artist in the fullest sense, someone who gardens, makes poems out of her garden, and makes her books by hand. And Lax, you know, wrote everything out by hand – and his handwriting, so clear and childlike – is an integral part of the poems.

JG: John, one final question before we turn to your poetry. We are contemporaries, born one year apart, and so share the great cultural crises of our time-the Vietnam War and Civil Rights Movement. I see from you visits to Vietnam and your membership in the Fellowship of Reconciliation, an international group that espouses peace through non-violence and compassion, that the Vietnam War has left an indelible mark on you. It seems as if you are willing to do whatever one man can do to undo the damage we did to the Vietnamese during the war years. Do you think the burden and sorrow you still bear has impacted the kind of poetry you write?

JM: You remind me of what a pretender I am. It's people like Karma Tenzing Wangchuk and a man I knew at the National Coalition for the homeless who have really been marked and are undoing the damage.

I think of the torment Paul Celan lived and died with – being a German Jewish poet; or Jewish German poet. Having to use that language at that time. And here we are, I am, writing and speaking in the American language, which made itself horrid and unspeakable then and daily still compounds itself.

JG: John, on this mythos, this marchen, we are currently creating and living through, I see the first obstacle, the first gate-keeper: sometimes it's known as abstraction, sometimes as post-modernism, sometimes it's referred to as Language poetry. I'd like to begin with a poem you wrote in syllables (author produced, 2008):

the world is made of syllables

Technically, a syllable is a unit of organization for a sequence of speech/writing sounds, upon which words are built. But, it is not just words, it is actually the "world," that is constructed by syllables. The poem can be taken either self-referentially, that is, "the world" mentioned in the poem is made of syllables, or it may have a referent beyond the confines of language-that is to say, "the world" "outside" of the poem. Perhaps, this ambiguity is the strength of the poem.

Then, also from syllables, we have this poem:

a breath

a life

a breath

a life

a breath

a life

a breath

a life

The poem has its urgency and rhythm through repetition of two nouns: breath, life. Again, it is left indeterminate whether there is an alternation between the abstract-"life"-and the concrete "breath." There seems to be a balance struck between the two and the indeterminacy is again the poem's strength.

One final example from syllables:

ram

shackle

from

ran

shackle

from

ransack

sack

thou

bag

worm

house

Here we have a beautifully rendering in reversal, following backwards the history of
the word ramshackle to its earliest etymology in ransack. Then, you use ambiguity
to suggest that either you would like your house, which you compare to a bagworm,
which is a moth in its cocoon and from which it will emerge reborn in a new,
developed form, to also enter and emerge from such a cocoon "sack," or alternatively
you are cursing and dismissing the dismal house by "sacking" it. Again, we have a
self-enclosed energy field of words, a poem as object, or a reference to existents
"outside" the confines of the poem.

I think this ambiguity, this indeterminacy, distinguishes your work from your
acknowledged predecessors: Robert Lax, his mentor Ad Reinhardt, and Frank
Samperi. Let's briefly look at what can only be called abstraction in the works of
these forebears.

To begin with, Ad Reinhardt was an abstract expressionist painter best known for
his black paintings, which though monochrome were actually painted in different
shades of black, in rectangles, and which suggested that there was no absolute, nothing beyond. Ad Reinhardt is famous for his quote, "Art is Art. Everything else is
everything else." Reinhardt, as you know deeply influenced Robert Lax. Here's a
Lax poem that is reminiscent of a Reinhardt painting and entitled "Homage to
Reinhardt."

black

black

black

blue

blue

blue

black

black

black

black

blue

blue

blue

Obviously, just as in Reinhardt's paintings, the poem by Lax is totally abstract, totally language qua language.

Then, as a final example, let's look at one of Frank Samperi's poems from Day (copyright 1999 The Samperi Estate and Claudia Samperi-Warren).

no

ground

only

fire

and

spirit

In this poem, we see Samperi's "groundless" state of spirituality, or abstraction. There are a number of poems written in this mode, but in all fairness, I think you share with Frank Samperi a tendency to balance the concrete with the abstract. Here's a final Samperi poem (Lumen Gloriae, Grossman Publishers, 1973):

space

my state

                        down

                to

            a

                t

We can see here, as in your work, a conceptual art, a concrete art, yet some relationship to an "outside," as it were.

I would like to interject here a quote from Chilean poet Vincente Huidobro (cited in Haiku 21, Modern Haiku Press, 2011):

> The abstract should become concrete and the concrete abstract. That is to say, a perfect equilibrium should obtain between the two, because if the abstract keeps stretching you further towards the abstract, it will come apart in your hands, and sift through your fingers. The concrete, if made still more concrete, can perhaps serve you some wine to drink or furnish your parlor, but it can never furnish your soul. (pg. 15)

John, how would you define yourself and your work in regard to the above discussion of abstract/concrete projects of poetry? I suspect you don't care for self-definition or definition in general, but just as a matter of shedding light on your work, I would appreciate your opinion on this subject.

JM: I'm not sure how well that abstract/concrete dichotomy works-after all, "concrete" poetry is a kind of abstract art, or can be, anyway.

I prefer to think of Lax and Samperi as contemplative poets. In Lax's case, the repetition can sometimes be an invocation of the thing – he's Adam naming the world. It's a poetry of realization, as you see in his poem about "lifting/one stone"- the saying is the doing of it- he has a primal sense of language. Other times, the repetition is mantra- or prayer-like, and some of his poems are dialogues with himself, an attempt to puzzle things through in the simplest language possible. (Remember, too, the poems emerge from his journals as responses to life). Sometimes, he's being a comic bop blues singer, very playful.

Samperi has a very visual sense of the poem on the page. He was meticulous about this in his manuscripts. The word as apparitional, visionary (whereas Lax is more oriented towards the spoken).

In my own case, I suppose everything depends on the poem in quootions…

JG: John, we've passed the first threshold. Now, at least for me, we are facing the dragon of our mythos, and that is your tendency to part words into their roots and branches, or simply to divide them at times. Now, you are no longer a journeyer with me, but now represent the Wise Old Man of mythology for me.

So, let's begin with some works from arbor (author published, 2005). The first poem I'd like to look at is the following:

black

berry-

shoots

al

ready

thorned

The parting of "al" from "ready" seems reasonable here: even in their early stages the shoots, "all" or "al" of them, prepared, "ready" protected, "thorned. Then, if we turn to another from the same collection, you divide one word into its root and infinitive and in another such word you leave the word intact.

> drying
>
> my
>
> pepper
>
> mint
>
> &
>
> water
>
> ing
>
> pines

I can understand why you'd divide "water" and the continuation of the action of pouring by making "ing" a separate entity, but it's difficult to follow when you begin with "drying" and do not follow the same design. Dividing "pepper" "mint" also is reasonable because the etymology almost calls for it, as the two parts of the word have separate origins in language. Or, in this poem, it is difficult to discover the purpose of a partial word, really one letter in place of a word:

gardener

writing

w dirty hands

Of course, the poem can be read in such a way that the writer merely wrote "w" and has dirty hands and what word he was going to complete is left unstated. But, that seems a bit of a stretch. Is it merely an instance of reduced language, as you describe poetry in your seminal essay "The Neolithic (re)turn in poetry." Or, again in this poem, there is a sense in the division of a word:

night

table

eye

glasses

ros

ary

pocket

knife

I can see "ros" "ary" as understandable because the etymology of rosary stems from "rosa," as a garden of roses and the rosary is thus a garden of prayers.

Let's go forward in time and look at word divisions in your poems included in

o

r

d

i

n

a

r

y

f

o

o

l (author published, 2008)

I like this particular poem because it admits of multiple meanings and so the division of "an" from "other" has its own sense:

> winter
>
> coat
>
> & gloves
>
> he's
>
> an
>
> other
>
> sparrow

Here, the poem can be read to mean this man dressed for winter is an "other," from the presence of a "sparrow." But, then there is this interesting and arresting poem:

these

> woods
>
> sing

le

syl

lab

les

Put together again, we have what we started with: " the world is made of syllables."
On the other hand, the poem can be understood to say the woods sing: le syl lab les.
I find this poem to be a pristine example of concrete poetry: everything in it is true
to the world of the poem: everything is a single syllable and makes up a world!

Let me turn finally to one more poem that divides a word purposely:

breathes

on his

fire

that

little

ani

mal (ksana, Redmoon Press, 2011)

This poem is another instance of multiple means created by the fragmentation of
the poem into one word lines (with the one exception). Rather than mean a little
animal, it could very well read as breathing just a bit, smoothly, softly "that little"
on his fire. The fact is that the only animal that creates fire is the human animal
and so the poem rather places man in his proper perspective in the universe as that
"little animal." Further evidence of this would be the division of "animal" into "ani"
and "mal," because the only animal that is divided against itself (see Freud's
Civilization and its Discontents) is the human animal: so the break of "ani" and
"mal" visually represents this fact.

John, I've covered a great deal of ground in this discussion. I can use you now as
representative of the Wise Old Man of Jungian psychoanalysis to guide me through
your rationales for word divisions and interruptions in your poems.

JM: As Denise Levertov had it, every poem arises organically from experience, felt through, and sometimes the rhythm will be more visual, sometimes, more musical, sometimes more syntactic. One never knows in advance.

The English word comes apart into syllables, as the Chinese ideogram comes apart into its radical and other members. In both cases, roots matter. Hopkins thought of the single word as a fossil poem.

In Buddhism, there are mantras – the great compassion mantra – and those in the Lotus sutra. One archaic syllable after another. Reciting them takes one somewhere – Samadhi.

Certainly breaking the word apart slows the reading process, takes one out of ordinary time and somewhere else. And any poem must do this.

I'm a great fan of Andrew Welch's Roots of Lyric.

JG: Okay, John. I believe we've squared the circle, entered the inner sanctum or the center, temporal or otherwise. We have gathered and girded ourselves to enjoy the fruits of our labor, which is the promise of the mythos. Ezra Pound pointed to its direction in Canto LXXXI:

> What thou lovest well remains,
>
> > the rest is dross
>
> What thou lov'st well shall not be reft from thee
>
> What thou lov'st well is they true heritage

So, we have worked our way to the point where I feel we can now discuss the poems of yours that I love, simply and truly. Let me begin with one of my favorites of yours:

> this mushroom
>
> > its own
>
> > > moonlight (Ksana, Redmoon Press, 2011)

In one sense, mushrooms appear to spring up overnight, and so one literal reading of the poem could well be the phenomenon of the mushroom at night reflecting moonlight. Additionally, and more to the point is that the common white button mushroom is shaped like the moon and bears a luminescence much like soft moonlight: it radiates from within. This latter reading gives the poem a delicately drawn self-enclosure that is hard to resist. Another poem, using white light is another favored by me:

snow

part of the

milky way (Roadrunner, 9.1, 2009)

Again, this poem also allows for multiple readings. On the one hand, it is snowing and while this is viewed so, peripherally, is a part of the Milky Way. I appreciate the way the poem is shaped concretely to emulate the flow of the Milky Way, the flow of the snow falling. Finally, of course, we have the fact that snow (even though it would melt before it even came close to the Milky Way) is a part of it, part of our galaxy. While we're on white, how about this poem:

my retinas such tiny sails (Masks 3, 2010)

The whites of the eyes, visible to the naked eye in a shape similar to sails. That's all and that's enough. Of course, the retinas are the light sensitive portion of the eye and make seeing possible; they are what allow us from "inside" to sail off into the world. I find this to be a brilliant, miniature and meaningful poem.

Then there is the heart-wrenching poem

some pebbles-

my dear friend's

here (Tumulus, author published, 2006)

A tumulus is a burial mound and what makes this poem so poignant is the minuteness of the mound, just some pebbles, to mark the place of the remains of a dear friend.

Then, there is the bittersweet poem of poverty, such as that of Raskolnikov in Crime and Punishment,

a trailer home

window

dostoyevsky (Roadrunner, 11:1, 2011),

where it is quite possible that at the trailer window is a man weathered, beaten, bearded and has the understanding of men that Dostoevsky had.

Finally, I will finish with another of my favorite poems by John Martone that was published in Roadrunner, X.3, 2010):

> vulture my other side

So, John, have I read these poems of yours I most admire satisfactorily, and are any of them favorites of yours, too. If not, could you enumerate a few of your favorite poems in your remarkably prolific career as a poet?

JM: Jack, such a careful study of these poems, leaves me a bit embarrassed.

It's hard for me to answer your last question. I don't remember my poems very well, couldn't recite any for you. I think that's why I'm always making these little books- in order to put the poems away- to get them out of the way. I want the next poem to be the first one. To get it right for once! There are those two meanings of practice – as something one does to improve and as what one does constantly. One's always working at it.

Lorine Niedecker, you know, wouldn't give public readings of her work- Cid Corman persuaded her to read into this tape recorder once, but that was it- she worked and wrote her poems, and I don't think the people she worked for ever knew she was a poet (not that it would have meant anything to them). She knew the Way.

JG: John, after reading many of your books, I feel as if you have collected the entire universe within them, so that your oft- defined style as minimalism ends up being something of a misnomer. In the pages prior to the poems in ksana, you include the following poem:

A million

disparate

moments

make the

whole

-RobertLax

This poem certainly defines your art to a t.

However , there was a curious remark you made in dogwood& honeysuckle (Redmoon Press, 2004) after you mention you glued shards of china to a clay pot. You went on to say "broken things become devotions." I find much of the worlds you inhabit and examine in your work are broken-trailers, pebbles with holes, a splinter, a trillium that was, things gone or going, and you make of them a devotion.

Yet, for all that I feel a sorrow in your work; compassion, yes, but sorrow. It reminds me of when The Fool(and one of your pen names is Ordinary Fool) in Federico Fellini's La Strada tells Gelsomina, a woman who has no sense of self-worth and lives in servitude to The Strongman, Zampano, that everything and everyone has a purpose- even a pebble, even her. He says that if the pebble has no purpose then nothing has any purpose.

In the end, after Zampano kills The Fool, Gelsomina is so broken in spirit that she dies of a broken heart. Then, when Zampano, who has been looking for her finds out that she died, he gets drunk and in the dark of night goes to the sea's edge and lays in the sand crying without end, broken, knowing through loss that he had loved and wasn't capable of realizing it until it was too late.

I feel this broken-heartedness in you, too, in your work. It is palpable to me. It is not the wabi or sabi of Basho, who for me adopted this as an aesthetic; nor is characteristic of any of the major Japanese haijin we've all read. There's a genuine solitude, loneliness, grief in your work that is heart-wrenching to me. Is this true to you or am I projecting my own emotional life into yours?

JM: Jack, What you've done is really very moving and clear, you see what I would want one to see. And I think, you know, it is already an essay in its own right, and anything I might add would dilute it with my own self-importance.

REVIEWS

A Future Waterfall: Ban'ya Natsuishi's Modernism

Ban'ya Natsuishi, A Future Waterfall: 100 Haiku from the Japanese, second revised edition, Red Moon Press (PO Box 2461, Winchester VA 22604-1661, USA), 2004, ISBN 1-893959-46-5, US $ 12 .

Red Moon Press: Redmoonattoshentel.Net

Every man faces in two directions. To the past, he stands as a forebear. To the future, he stands as standard bearer. In either stance, he is an interpreter, for the past is always contested and the future is the temporary outcome. Every man is a modernist, in other words, willingly or no. Only those who know this are artists. The rest are dogmatists or iconoclasts.

The reissue last year (2004) of A Future Waterfall: 100 Haiku from the Japanese, by Red Moon Press, seen in this perspective, is an event of singular importance. It signals the success of the work. This signals that the reshaping of the past in terms of the present as performed by Mr. Natsuishi has struck a chord-atonal and sometimes discordant-in a wide audience. The question remains, though, as to what accounts for Mr. Natsuishi's widening influence in the world of modern poetry.

Though it is not the centerpiece of the book, or its best poem, the following poem might well stand as the book's credo:

I came away, abandoning

the Thousand-Year-Old Cedar

dandled by the storm

The poem works almost exclusively by allusion to a poem of Matsuo Basho written in the seventeenth century: the last night of the month, no moon:.. / Thousand-year-old-cedars besieged by a storm Mr. Natsuishi 'poem inscribes within it what is essential to modernism:. a proclamation of independence from tradition in the rejection of the earlier poem and its submissive posture to the grandeur of nature, yet simultaneously the preservation of that tradition in referencing the old poem in the new The old style and subject is "abandoned," yet devotedly retained. Mr.

Natsuishi sets off on his own path in this poem, yet he strikingly adheres to Basho's advice to poets to not imitate the ancient masters, but to seek what they sought. And what was it the ancient masters sought, if not an original relationship to nature.

Having abandoned the ancient loci of tradition, where has Mr. Natsuishi's path led. Partly, his path has progressed along a road that has been in the building for the last century. His haiku, like that of others in the twentieth century, has grown by including within itself a greater scope of subject as new terrain than the form allowed in its more formalized past. Mr. Natsuishi writes on subjects such as television, sex, newspapers, bureaucrats, electric wires, and cultures undreamt of by the ancients. There is nothing exactly new in this approach. Yet, Mr. Natsuishi brings originality to this process of inclusion in the art of haiku hitherto unseen.

A mother sucks

her baby's cock

amid a sea of mulberry leaves

At first sight, this poem strikes the reader as shocking in its use of incestuous imagery. Yet the poem in style is really quite conventional. Conventional haiku has been said to be the juxtaposition of images, whereby its two phrases so placed shed light on one another and thereby create a new, third element of meaning. This poem utilizes this technique in its manner and introduces no technical innovation. The images chosen are quite smart, though. For what is spring if not the lush, reproductive urge of nature that is so luxuriant as to overwhelm discreet human order. That is implied in the poem by a mother sucking her baby's cock. The procreant urge of the world knows no borders, no negatives. This is further conveyed in the haiku by the categorical confusion in the phrase "sea of. leaves," for sea and leaves, like mother having sex with an infant, are categories that do not properly belong together. If the reader realizes that Mr. Natsuishi does not mean the incest literary, but as the shock to decorum . that is spring, then the poem would be better understood Again, he conveys this shock of spring to the moral sensibility in the following:. Assaulting / a formally dressed old woman / the wisteria Spring, my friends, is not decent and we should not poeticize about it in saccharine terms.

A slippery sex organ

and another

give birth to gold

This poem without a seasonal reference is a good example of how Mr. Natsuishi's aesthetic of using keywords-here sex-in its place can be used to creative ends. This poem can almost be said to be a meta-haiku, for the poem is about adding two elements and arriving at a third, which the poem utilizes in its construction The adjective "slippery" is well-chosen:. it gives the impression of seals swimming, of moist living beings playing together, and by association is indirectly associated with the waters of spring and life. The finale is fine, like alchemy. Out of our love, sloppy wet or not, comes the most precious element, gold. And, out of his devotion for this art of joining two elements till they fire into a third, Mr. Natsuishi is the archetypal alchemist.

Cherry blossoms fall:

newspapers

suck in a great deal of blood

He is also very sensitive. If you hold these two contrasting images contained in this poem in your mind, you would fairly burst with the hurt and beauty of the world simultaneously existing in you. Cherry blossoms, white or red depending on what kind, in appearance resemble the newsprint and blood conveyed in the second image. There is also a similarity in the texture of petals and newsprint. Of course, newspapers do absorb a tremendous amount of news about death and war all over the globe almost as if it were

natural, as if the absorbent quality of paper were responsible, or as if the medium were alive and thirsted for such tabloid material. If the two images are held in suspension, though, the tender beauty and gory nature of the world seem to hold one another in an embrace, each looking in the other's face for love, explanation, and understanding, till the mind holding them together fairly screams for release.

I diarrhea

electric wires, birds, fireworks

and clouds

He can also be crass and mystical at the same time, containing within himself the whole world (for what world is separable from the perceiving mind) and letting it fly out not able to hold it back anymore, somewhat like Walt Whitman who contained multitudes and miracles.

On television

a large root dances

Manhattan below zero

Or he can be incisive and detached, as an outside observer can be of a foreign culture. In sudden, deep freeze, the frenetic activity seen on television in New York City is much like a giant, exposed nerve or root retracting or twitching to keep . alive against an unfamiliar threat And New York City is and always has been unrelentingly stern and harsh to its inhabitants and all its sentient life: For three hundred years / blue black blue black / New York.

I write a haiku of darkness

to the painter

who keeps a Pharaoh's dog

But, he is always immensely inventive and deeply aware of what is the essence of haiku. Here, we have a poem that neither caters to the syllable count of classical haiku nor to its requirement of a seasonal reference. Yet, the result is haiku par excellence. "Darkness," another use of the keyword concept of Mr.Natsuishi, is a universal experience, as meaningful to human beings as are the seasons and as rhythmic and recurring. This nocturne relies for its force on the phrase "pharaoh's dog, "and what better expression for darkness than reference to a dead culture and an animal deity, Annubis, who led the souls of the dead to the underworld. The poem uses allusion well and by this device gives depths to darkness that is surprising in a poem of so few words. It is a poem lovingly painted with the black of hieroglyphs.

The estuary where

neither the rising nor setting sun's visible

I call mother

He is finally truly tender and loving. This poem of absence conveys in few words a man's true feelings towards his mother. Indeed, the sentiment the poem contains can be said to be the experience of all grown men towards their mothers. What was the fond source of all future unfolding becomes invisible, no longer present. An "estuary," small but feeding the greater rush of life towards the boundless world, there somehow, lending its influence from the beginning, but lost as it joins the rest of time, and dearly remembered. I do not know if Mr. Natsuishi's mother has passed on, as the poem may suggest, but in the life of a man a mother is always a poignant absence that cannot be found in the light of day.

Besides the many poems contained in this book of modern haiku, the editor, Mr. Jim Kacian, has included a number of interviews and addresses featuring Ban'ya Natsuishi. This inclusion of the prose pieces of Mr. Natsuishi is perspicacious and adds an important dimension to the work. It affords those readers who are unfamiliar with Mr. Natsuishi a chance to hear his remarks on the history of haiku, to hear him comment on the difference between seasonal words used in classical haiku and his own creation of a replacement for it in the concept of keyword, and to hear his thoughts on the subject of modernism in poetry in general. Having read the poems, the prose pieces cast light on them for the reader, and the poems can then be reread in a new light. The structure of the book is much like a haiku, two parted, with each section contributing towards a synthesis.

We are grateful to Mr. Natsuishi for this work and for Mr. Kacian for making it available.

The Cultivated Field: Tateo Fukutomi's Straw Hat

The world should not lie useless. It should be scooped up in the hands and sifted through the fingers and scored with the ridges of the palm. The whole world is fertile, even the world of memory, even the world of the departed. That is what cultivation serves: it enriches the soil and the self in one fell act. In the art of cultivation, a man eventually takes on the contours of what he has lovingly touched, until it is impossible to say where the world begins and the man ends. A man whose life has been devoted to preparing the field finds himself disappearing into the earth only to be returned by the earth to himself. He knows kinship with the things of the earth. He finds that the world of spirit springs from the soil. If he should travel, he finds he has never really moved. If he should die, he finds that he has never left home.

Recently reading Straw Hat by Tateo Fukutomi, I was struck by the ordinary collage of things that go into the assembling of a book: the paper itself, the three lines of each haiku in English, the tall vertical columns of the Japanese alongside, the ink drawings, stitching, binding. The very physical features of the book were alive. Everything pronounced itself as present. This is an achievement, for the purpose of a book of haiku, like the purpose of art generally, is to make us see what we have so often regarded that we have grown too benumbed to experience it freshly. This is the first order of cultivation: the making visible of the world that has fallen into despair. Mr. Fukutomi opens:

Summer recedes from view

ribs gather

in a corner of the inlet

We witness the appearance of autumn, without its being named, by the mention of another season receding. This is the essence of autumn, this "receding," this absence of fullness, this absence of presence. Autumn is depicted most validly by its absence. This is a brilliant rendition of a classical seasonal theme in the art of haiku. Mr. Fukutomi adds to absence in the haiku by his presentation of the fleshless in "ribs" in the second line. The whole solidifies an autumnal impression in the reader that is not soon forgotten.

A white-aproned woman

A black cow

A couple

Mr. Fukutomi also draws clean, clear lines with ease, as in the poem above. He works sparsely, in black and white, and intimates a world of complexity. This is the second order of cultivation: to open up the unseen corridors of a world grown uncertain of itself. In the haiku, distinctions are shown to rely on other distinctions and thus to be the sides of one body. The woman in white and the cow of black are only understood in opposition to one another, which is another way of saying in relationship to one another. They are related, closely, intimately, a "couple." There is no black without white. No woman without cow. This is the way the world works, according to Mr. Fukutomi: all things are related, as all things rely for their definition on the definition of other things.

My wife isn't here to see me off

a red bouquet

scatters in the sky

Here we have the abandon of love even in abandonment. If we do not express our love to a chosen, we express it to the world entire, casting our sensuality to the sky. Or, is it anger that the poet feels? Or is anger love, anyway? The sunset is a red bouquet resplendent in the sky. Where the poet's wife is missing, the natural world fills the void, offering all of the solicitation the poet could ever ask for. The world wishes off the cultivated traveler, for he has imbued it with his love.

Insects fall

Into a battered pot

Left deep in the mountains

What world would not respond to such sensitivity and love as the poet expresses in this haiku. It is the eye of god a man has who sees the spent life of the small forms of the infinite. An abandoned pot, a sign of civilization, deep in the mountains becomes a burial urn accidentally to insects whose lives have been spent in bringing the next generation into existence. What sound do they make when they fall? The same sound that the discarded pot makes, the sound that all things make as they leave off their shapes and one time purpose and enter the greater rhythm of all things.

In a field

where buried axe-heads surface

tree spirits assemble

Things are joined forever that have interacted. The spirits of felled trees will always accompany the reemergence of the axe-heads that chopped them down. When what we have done, our tools and their uses, emerges we find our responsibility. This is the third order of cultivation: to show us the world we have made and its consequences. It is our form of justice.

Blue-green grasses

shimmering in June

President Kennedy is dead

Martin Luther King's death

clover flowers softly covering

rice paddies

We needn't be reminded of what we have done, must we? Mr. Fukutomi was in the United States of America at the time of the two fateful assassinations of the two great men of these haiku. He makes for each man an eternal sepulcher, of such shape and tenderness as his mind can fashion. He takes license with the date of President Kennedy's death only to overpower the mind with discrepancy: for the shimmering beauty of blue-green June grass held in juxtaposition to dire death is unbearable to the imagination. It doesn't make sense and it is not meant to make sense. The fields unspeakably beautiful, the death unspeakably horrible, breaks the heart holding them in one breath.

It is likewise in his memorial to Martin Luther King: the beauty of clover overrunning a harvested rice paddy, the gorgeous colors and softness compares not at all to the death of a national leader of peace. The mind would stop this overrunning of nature, this refusal of time to stop even at such tragic moments, the face of beauty in the face of horror. And yet so it is and the poet makes us weep anew and take responsibility.

Memory of the atomic bomb

every time the wind pulls off my hat

I put it back on

We are defenseless sometimes in the face of what we have done, as defenseless as a man trying to ward off a memory of catastrophic proportions by placing his hat back on his head to protect it. It is tragi-comic this haiku. The winds of memory are in every fresh gust. They surround us. We cannot shake free of them. What must it have been like for a man to have felt a sudden overpowering wind one morning that first grabbed his hat off his head and the next minute removed his beloved city from the face of the earth? Every slight foreboding in every single moment of life will trigger an automatic response of a fear out of proportion to the moment. It is dreadful to think about. Yet, it is our responsibility to think about it.

A newborn's eyes open

Shortening the march

Of human evolution

Lest I forget to mention it, another dimension of cultivation is that it brings us to our glory. We are perfect, the poet tells us, and pure. There is need to "march," no need for all the schemes devised by humankind to achieve perfection in a distant time. The time is now. The newborn's eyes open on our original face, before our mother and father were born, when we were the all that is: they see, and in them and all new things we experience, that participation mystique in which we are the world.

A stone bench for no reason

dark falls

among cypresses

Perhaps, the single most important function of cultivation is to show us the beauty of the world at rest. After the work is done, after the simple stone of the field is hewn into the human universe, it resumes its proper place once more in the world as a stone. It was always a bench and a stone and now that cultivation has lifted it out of the prima materia of the universe uncreated, we see it in its pristine nature. It has "no reason," except what we imagine and build. Having lifted it out of primal unity and given it distinction, then all distinctions arise as unity once more. The meaningless cool, dark stone slab is darkness and cypresses. They unite in dark beauty for the mind of light.

So, it is with the physical construction of Straw Hat, which, by the way, has two publications. We would like to take this time to thank the two publishers, Jin Shionoya Kaiteishinsha, in the year 2000, and Estapa Editions, Coulimer, France, in the year 2004. We would also like to thank the translators, Kate van Houten and Shelley Dauvillier, and Jonathon Reinhardt. Thanks also go to Matsutani for the wonderful ink drawings contained in the 2004 edition of Straw Hat.

Finally, we express our deep gratitude to the poet, Tateo Fukutomi, for his offerings to the world. Without them, the world would be that much less understood and appreciated.

Part I

The Romance of Primitivism: Tohta Kaneko's *Ikemono fuei*

For those unfamiliar with Tohta Kaneko, he is the august age of 93 years and his career in Japan as educator, scholar, poet and critic spans 75 of those years. He is considered amongst the most important literary and cultural innovators of postwar modern haiku. He served as the President of the Modern Haiku Association from 1983 to 2000. Over his career, he was the recipient of amongst others, The Medal of Honor, Purple Ribbon (1988), The Order of Rising Sun, Fourth Class (1995), and Person of Cultural Merit, Japan (2008). He is also the author of fourteen books of haiku.

In 1999, Mr. Kaneko gave a speech before the Modern Haiku Association entitled "Poetic Composition on Living Things (translated as *Ikemonofuei,* the latter a word coined by Mr. Kaneko, published by Redmoon Press, 2011). Rather than beginning with an epigram, Mr. Kaneko began with a poem of his own, a poem that in its structure, images, and meaning essentially sums up all that follows in his delivery to the audience. Here is the poem:

> splendid field of gravestones
>
> labia uncovered
>
> the village sleeps

Because the poem has specific references, allusions, and meanings related to Japanese history, the translators included end notes to elucidate the poem's significance. The poem was written in 1958 in a small village in Nagasaki. It was a fishing village, and after the atomic bombing of Nagasaki, there were no fish as a result of radiation fallout and so the village was starved. The locale was filthy, squalid, women walked about without undergarments, their genitals exposed. The only pristine place was the graveyard with its "splendid" gravestones. The final line, "the village sleeps," is meant to convey a zombie-like atmosphere of death in life.

What is central to this poem is its sense of what Mr. Kaneko calls *shakaisei haiku* (social consciousness/awareness in haiku) and *taido*, the importance of an author's "stance" in relation to society (See Dr. Richard Gilbert's Introduction for further elucidation). For Mr. Kaneko, haiku that lacks social awareness and an author's stance vis-à-vis society is simply a vapid product, worthless, untrustworthy. Of the many points Mr. Kaneko makes in his address, this is one we as English language practitioners of haiku do well to bear in mind, because for the most part we have viewed these terms as too polemical, too ideological to be included in our haiku (this will be discussed later in greater detail).

As Mr. Kaneko lived through most of the twentieth century, he personally experienced and participated in the hallmark shifts in the art of haiku in Japan. This lends an air of intimacy to the subject, as well as the strength of personal witness. Thus, Mr. Kaneko begins his address with opposition to long-held conventions in Japanese haiku, which were disseminated by Takaham Kyoshi, a student of Masaoka Shiki, and who edited *Hototogisu* after Shiki's death; the three terms he opposes are *kachofuei* (poetic com- position on birds and flowers), *kyakkanshansei* (an objective sketch), and *yuki teikei*, (" a fixed form with season words," page 19, Ibid). Mr. Kaneko boldly says none of these long-cherished terms have much to do with content in haiku and are merely catchphrases.

Although it might seem to belabor the point, Mr. Kaneko makes clear that to write only of birds and flowers as representations of nature is too restrictive and unnecessarily narrows the view of a poet of what is nature. It excludes all other living things, including human beings, who, for Mr. Kaneko, are like other living beings (what he calls *ikimono*). And, oddly, he refers to this excepting of human beings in haiku as a corrupting influence of modernism, insofar as it separates man from nature, sets them at strife. While there is admittedly some truth to this interpretation, it is based on a view that nature preceded culture and at this time, this golden age, man and nature were united. However, as there must be a threshold at which culture is said to exist, it is really only at this moment that nature can be said to exist, since prior thereto there was no conceptual division. In this sense, it can be said that culture preceded nature and there was no nature prior when man and nature were in unison.

Mr. Kaneko charges Kyoshi with upholding "obedience to nature" as a condition of writing haiku of the old order (of birds and flowers). He points out that this privileging of "nature," as one of the terms of the equation of nature versus man or other living things is an imbalanced position, a metaphysics, and one that distorts the parity of opposites (if, indeed, they are opposites). As Mr. Kaneko says:

I think this idea of obedience is the crux of the problem: we need not harbor any idea of obedience. Human beings are living things, cockroaches are living things, tigers are living things-there is no need to obey the other. Human beings have parity; that is, we are equal an equivalent as *ikimono* (living things, living beings). (Ibid, page 21).

Again, Mr. Kaneko attributes this mistaken view to modernism, which relies on "categorization" for the sake of knowledge. Needless to say, Mr. Kaneko is relying on what he believes to be an unmediated knowing that preceded language as a technology of categorization (and this subject will be discussed at length later on).

Mr. Kaneko's introduction to the haiku world was through his father, who wrote haiku and held haiku meetings at their home. One of the members of this group was Mizuhara Shuoshi, a man who wrote an influential essay entitled "Truth in Nature and Truth in Literature," 1931). Mr. Shuoshi's position was that subjectivity was an important factor in life and should be included in haiku. This idea went against the grain of the dominant haiku culture, led by members of Hototogitsu Journal. In response to this seminal essay, Kyoshi advocated what he called the "objective sketch" (*kyakkanshasei*). And this is a momentous realization for those of use educated in the belief that it was Shiki, the inventor of haiku, who created the objective sketch-from-life theory of haiku. According to Mr. Kaneko, Shiki had just referred haiku to *shasei,* a sketch, rather than insisting on "objectivity."

It has been a grave mistake on the part of English language haiku poets to believe for so long that Shiki required "objective" sketches of nature. This misunderstanding has nurtured half-a-century of haiku poets. If we think of the word "sketch," we have a better understanding of what Shiki meant by *shasei;* a sketch is quickly done-usually-and uses few lines to convey and capture the essence of something. Shiki, as Mr. Kaneko notes, wrote about all things that interested him, subjective and objective.

Hekigoto, a disciple of Shiki's, traveled throughout Japan advocating that haijin should write what they directly felt and experienced. This is a far cry from the Shiki we have been used to reading about in the many Anglo-American journals of the past fifty years.

During the period in question noted above, when free-form haiku and subjective haiku appeared on the scene, it was an exciting time. Kawahigashi Hekigoto promulgated the form of free-rhythm haiku, and amongst his students was the avant-garde poet Santoka Taneda , while Ozaki Hosai was a follower of Shuoshi's subjective and free-verse style.

Having had his tutelage in his father's home where discussions about haiku were often heated, passionate, and though intelligent, somewhat wild, Mr. Kaneko always retained this understanding of haiku as the art of an ordinary human being, with the feelings of a human being. He was from the beginning indifferent to ideologies and polemics.

Looking for a poet to model himself on, Mr. Kaneko chose Kobayashi Issa. Issa fit his idea of what was most human; he believed that Issa, because he was not of a high enough caste to be a master of haikai-no-renga, and because he had suffered so much, having lost his ancestral home to the machinations of his stepmother, and having lost his wife and four children to death, Issa possessed the most developed sense of a living being (*ikimono*). Mr. Kaneko believed that Issa obtained the greatest degree of sensitivity to life, what Mr. Kaneko calls "raw perceptions of living beings." (ikimono *kankaku*). In Issa, Mr. Kaneko saw the primeval image of a human being, a beggar on the streets of Edo, much as Lear saw in Edgar "Is man no more than this? Consider him well. Thou ow'st the worm no silk, the beast no hide, the sheep no wool, the cat no perfume. Here's three on's are sophisticated. Thou art the thing itself; unaccommodated man is no more than such a poor, bare, forked animal as thou art.

It should be borne in mind, that Issa, living in the 18th Century, was without formal education, and his haiku are written in unassuming, innocent, artless, unadorned fashion. This is his strength, as well as his limitation. Many of his poems are poignant, and many are sentimental as a result of direct, unstudied articulation.

Mr.Kaneko, however, was a scholar, who before choosing Issa as a model, familiarized himself with the Chinese and Japanese classics, from Iio Sogi to haikai and renga and through Basho. So, his decision to write in the wild, ordinary language of Issa was more of an adoption of a narrative style than a natural manifestation of an untutored spirit. And, as will shortly be seen, this poses something of a problem, something of an illusion.

Mr. Kaneko takes on faith the idea of a golden age of man, when he lived in the forest, where he could develop and did develop the raw perception of living beings. As he says, "to put it another way, there is a world of sensitivity nurtured in those places where we touch the earth, living in forests…I think there is a kind of instinctual raw perception." (Ibid, pg. 40).

Mr. Kaneko goes on to suggest that life in the forest developed a "good nature" in human beings and he believes this is instinctive sensitivity. He contrasts this with the life that man developed in societies once he left the forest. Then, man became rapacious; from the innately good man degenerates to the defiled, where people harm others to get what they want.

The binary opposition that Mr. Kaneko creates between nature/forest and society/man-made is one in which he privileges the first and denigrates the latter. This is a thinking typical of the Western Metaphysical tradition. We are reminded in Mr. Kaneko's analysis of the 17th and 18th century Western notion of the noble savage, where pre-civilized man was an idealized indigene, another, an outsider who bears none of the taints of culture. This idealized picture of "nature's gentleman" was part of the period's sentimentality.

The idea that in a state of nature humans are essentially good is often attributed to the 3rd Earl of Shaftesbury, a Whig supporter of constitutional monarchy. In his Inquiry Concerning Virtue (1699), Shaftesbury had postulated that the moral sense in humans is natural and innate and based on feelings rather than resulting from the indoctrination of a particular religion. Shaftesbury was reacting to Thomas Hobbes's justification of royal absolutism in his Leviathan, Chapter XIII, in which he famously holds that the state of nature is a "war of all against all" in which men's lives are "solitary, poor, nasty, brutish, and short". The notion of the state of nature itself derives from the republican writings of Cicero and of Lucretius, both of whom enjoyed great vogue in the 18th century, after having been revived amid the optimistic atmosphere of Renaissance humanism (Wikipedia on the Noble Savage).

By the 19th Century, with the scientific and technological advances made in the Anglo-American world, the idea of the noble savage began to wane as an alternative to what was considered the inevitable progressive development of humanity within the confines of society. Actually, there was some question at this time as to whether the indigenous peoples of the earth would survive the expansions of the Western world due to colonialism. The idea of the gentleman of nature was replaced by the socially achieved modern human being to the extent that a rampant racism developed, even in anthropologists, whose aim was to study "primitive" societies without imposing Western civilization's views on them.

A number of authors, including William Golding, the film maker Stanley Kubrick, Australian anthropologist Roger Sandall, and archeologist Lawrence H. Keeley, who has criticized a "widespread myth" that "civilized humans have fallen from grace from a simple primeval happiness, a peaceful golden age" by uncovering archeological evidence that he claims demonstrates that violence prevailed in the earliest human societies. Keeley argues that the "noble savage" paradigm has warped anthropological literature to political ends. (War Before Civilization: The Myth of the Peaceful Savage (Oxford, University Press, 1996, page 5).

For Mr. Kaneko, the desire to escape the impurities of society has led many haiku poets to be wanderers, "settled wanderers," he calls them, because while they remain in society they do not adopt society's values. Since many of the haikai and renga poets had patrons, this state of affairs could actually be achieved. The poets were freed to develop their sensitivities and their poetics, without struggling to survive.

It was different for Issa. He was unable to become a professional haiku poet and so lived on the meager coins he received from strangers. Yet, he maintained an equilibrium, a joy:

> spring arrives-
>
> not reduced to begging
>
> after fifty years

Issa referred to himself as a wild, ordinary man, which Mr. Kaneko translates as *arabonpu,* which he took to mean vulgar or rough, but also free. For Tohta Kaneko, Issa, having grown up as the child of a farmer, kept that purity that comes from being in touch with the earth: Kaneko says, "to my mind, he grew up receiving the essence of the soil. (Ibid, page 51).

To demonstrate that Issa's sensitivity remained with him throughout life as a result of being a "wild, ordinary man," Mr. Kaneko sites two poems that illustrate Issa's gentleness, even after a life lived in such hardship.

> on a straw doll
>
> a louse on its back

floating away

Mr. Kaneko reads this poem to mean that Issa had removed a louse from a young girl's body, placed it on a doll's back, and floating down river. Mr. Kaneko goes so far as to suggest that if those who seize markets and wage war were forced to read Issa's gentle poems, their lust for power might diminish.

Tohta Kaneko summarizes his view of Issa by saying that his raw perception of a living being enabled him and would enable us, if we but followed his example, to connect us with all living beings. This is the world of haiku. This is Tohta Kaneko's view of modern haiku.

"Begone, Kyoshi! Banzai, Modern Haiku Association!"

Part II

Shiso: The Embodied Thinking of Tohta Kaneko

In The Future of Haiku: An Interview with Kaneko Tohta (Redmoon Press, 2011), Mr. Kaneko introduces a word of his own coinage, shiso, which, while related to the English word ideology has the additional meaning of existentially (physically) embodied thinking. For Mr. Kaneko, ideology per se, unless it is lived bodily is deceitful, empty. As he explains, "no, not an '-ism.'" I am reminded by his remarks of a haiku by Paul Pfleuger, Jr, a haiku that corresponds quite closely to what Mr. Kaneko has in mind (that intellectualized ideologies are superficial):

Isms with our clothes on

For Mr.Kaneko, life moves by instinct and this he equates with freedom. It's nama, a raw thing, or, perhaps better expressed a "fresh" thing, without forethought, without plan. It is a unfettered existence, and, in that regard, pure. Of course, living in such an unrestricted fashion can cause great harm to others and Mr. Kaneko acknowledges this fact. Yet, in describing the life of the poet Issa, Mr. Kaneko notes that while he was a man of earthy desires, when his instinct for wild, fresh life interacted with other living things, "an extraordinarily beautiful (sensitive) response is apparent." (Ibid, supra, page 23). Mr. Kaneko concedes that he learned how to live by Issa's example and like Issa he developed a sense that all things were on an equal level to him; from Issa, Mr. Kaneko learned not to discriminate.

There are a number of implications that arise from such a position as that noted above. Firstly, Mr. Kaneko learned from Issa to disregard the authority of the saijiki (an official volume of poems related to those written on the seasons) and their kigo (seasonal references) that was dominated by centers of learning in Edo and Kyoto. That Issa was able in the 18th Century to say I write as I please was quite unusual and enabled Mr. Kaneko to advocate writing haiku by choosing kigo of one's own choosing, not accepted as handed down from on high. It also led Mr. Kaneko, as President of the Modern Haiku Association, to create haiku of mukigo (no-season words) as an alternative. This was a radical break from tradition, especially in so formalized a society as Japan.

Of course, the most obvious repercussion of a wild life would be, as Professor Richard Gilbert points out in the interview is that Westerners would view this as living like an "animal," without conscience, anti-social. Mr. Kaneko clarifies wild, raw experience by including within its framework "an intellectual component, as well. (Ibid, supra, page 31). For Mr. Kaneko haiku must be "graphic," and "vivid,"and that would satisfy his terminology of the raw, visceral experience.

Mr. Kaneko offers three of his haiku that exemplify his idea of perceptually rawness. The first is stunningly sensual, blending the cover and color of night with the sliding and touching of carp: the words he chooses to describe the "scene" are vivid and lively.

valley, carp:

pushing and jolting

pleasure of night

The second example requires some explication. It expresses, in an elusive fashion, the tender tie between the poet and his mother and takes place in "mountain country," which is where Mr. Kaneko grew up. While it apparently is critical of the poet, because he did not follow his father's profession of medicine, but instead chose to be a haijin, the familiarity of mother and son is palpable:

summer mountain count

mother there calls me

"good-for-nothing"

The third and final example given of the poetry of an ordinary human being is explicit about birth and connects it closely to excreting. Again, it is raw, natural, yet loving.

My long-lived mother delivered me as if a shit

Mr. Kaneko is questioned as to whether, because of its brevity, haiku is limited in what it can express. He answers that the question is posed in a prosaic mind-set and in such a mind-set haiku cannot fulfill what prose can. However, he differentiates between this way of looking at haiku and suggests that if haiku is considered as a rhythmic form with a kire, or cutting word between the two parts of a haiku, then the cutting (in space and time) creates blendings of two images that can evoke all the multiplicity of meanings that prose achieves. In 1946, Kuwabara Takeo wrote a famous essay entitled "Haiku as a Second –class Art," precisely because he believed it couldn't convey the richness of ideas of other art forms and Mr. Kaneko decried this idea, assuming one had acclimated oneself to the haiku form.

As a corollary to the question of what it means to be a "wild, ordinary being," there is the question of social consciousness and what part it plays in haiku. Mr. Kaneko associates social consciousness with what he calls taido (stance). It relates to what he discussed earlier as "ideology," and partakes of a human being's interaction with society, with how they face society. For Mr. Kaneko haiku is born in this inter-face, without preconceived notions of society or experience, by what he terms an "autonomous self." As the idea of an autonomous self is contrary to a human being as a member of a society, as a species-being, as the self can never be truly "autonomous," dependent as it is on environs of all sorts, the definition given of this concept by Mr. Kaneko will be informative:

The autonomous self- an aspect of the zokei-ron theory which attempts to situate the self between subject and object; to reorient the haiku poet away from both kyakkanshasei-the objective sketch-and the radically subjective –which implies another form of self-dependence. To properly compose new haiku, one must be 'positioned' between subjective and objective: "The sense of existence is much more important than existence, because we should inquire as to the reality of the compositional expression of independent mind (independent-mindedness)." (Kaneko Tohta, Collected Works, IV, p. 261.)

The interview turns to Mr. Kaneko's wartime experiences, when he was a naval accounting officer on the Truk Atoll (where he became a prisoner-of-war for over a year). During this period of his life, he saw how some of those who fought for the Japanese were either conscripted Koreans, or criminals, those without soldierly status. When the Americans bombed the Atoll, all the rice that was stored was burned and soon many, particularly the non-soldiers, died of starvation. Of course, Mr. Kaneko was against the war and described war straightforwardly as "slaughter on a massive scale. It is genocide (The Future of Haiku, page 82.

Mr. Kaneko wrote haiku while he was a prisoner of war and kept faith with those who died as the unfortunate dead. Here is an example of one of his poems, a fitting, poignant tribute to the fallen. The poem was written when Mr. Kaneko was returning by ship after release from a POW camp.

the disappearing wake-

leaving behind the scorched fire

of unmarked graves

Mr. Kaneko notes that the heat described refers to both tropical islands, as well as to "burning heaven."

Mr. Kaneko wrote another haiku referencing the war, but this one is personal, a reproach to his father, who was right-wing and a war supporter.

my father's pro-war stance

I won't admit even today-

living in the summer

Tohta Kaneko also discusses his visit after the war to Nagasaki and surprisingly informs us that not only was there the atomic bomb's devastation to cope with, but there was also the persecution of hidden Christians, who lived on Amakusa (nearby Nagasaki) that he had to absorb. For him, it was a double and deep tribulation. Here is the haiku he penned to describe this double torment:

of my home country

the statue of Maria's tears-

A-bomb memorial

In the final question posed to him, Mr. Kaneko is asked to comment on the future of haiku. He notes that modern technologies- texting, blogs, and the like naturally lent themselves to brief expressions and so he thought the future of haiku, as the briefest of poems, had a bright future, the only future, perhaps. He even goes on to say that young people may prefer the stylism of Tsukeku and Tsukeai (short form poetry of call-and-response); or, twitter, which he says is similar to renku. Finally, as young people like music, Mr. Kaneko surmises that perhaps they will be drawn to the rhythmic aspect of haiku. For him, there are numerous possibilities open for the future of haiku and he is most optimistic in this regard.

To get sense of the depth of feeling Mr. Kaneko is capable of, I offer here one of his poems celebrating the sacrifice of the unfortunate dead of WWII:

island of martyrdom-

in twilight

a rusting ax

VIEWS

Shadow Play: The World of Robert Boldman

Let us begin where Robert Boldman's book of haiku everything I touch (Redmoon Press, 2011) begins.

JANUARY FIRST

the fingers of the prostitute cold

The very first day of the year, a beginning, capitalized to emphasize the start of something; but where does the poet place the *locus*? Not in the expected coldness of the season, nor in the cold extremities of a person outside (physiologically the extremities are the first to feel cold because blood moves inward in such temperature to protect the innermost organs), but in the fingers of the socially degraded, kept on a cold corner, the prostitute, one who abjectly doesn't "reproduce" in a "productive" society. It is synecdoche; the part (fingers) that strikes us: it is reductive, mirroring the status of the prostitute. It is an accurate, unflinching, unsentimental poem. We can hear echoes of the monk's words in the beginning of Rashomon (Akira Kurosawa, 1950), "I must not believe that men are so sinful." And, we are invited, as in *Rashomon,* after a woodcutter (a perjurer and thief) takes home a baby they find abandoned in the rain to raise in his own poor home, to feel with the monk, "I'm grateful to you. Because, thanks to you, I think I will be able to keep my faith in men." But, is it that simple for Robert Boldman? Is the human heart, corrupt, vagrant, flawed warm enough to heat the world?

Judging from the second poem in everything i touch, the answer is neither yes nor no; and (N.B) it is from this poem that the book takes its title:

a cold night

like the wind   letting go

of everything i touch

Mr. Boldman recognizes that human beings feel, they reach out, they touch everything, things have special significance for them; that is how we are; but he says in admonition, in gently teaching my example, let go though you are touched and touch. Be "like the wind," never stopping anywhere. This is reminiscent of the teaching of *Tilopa,* who taught the essence of how to live: "No thought, no reflection, no analysis, no cultivation, no intention; let it settle itself." Difficult? To be sure. But, what are the alternatives? Every thought, every attachment, every goal, every desire, is based on the illusion of a "self," of a little man inside (as Ludwig Wittgenstein claimed was how we saw the mind and why we lived in such confusion), impermeable, intrinsic, essential. Again, like the first poem, this poem is simple, untaxed with moralism, without the piousness that some refer to as the "stink of Zen." ("Lecture of Zen," found at Alan Watts at deoxy.org).

The earth is frozen hard, can tear your flesh; this is our background, our theater. You've all seen *Nature* documentaries where survival sometimes turns the snow soaking blood from a polar bear (white=purity?) rending the flesh of an unsuspecting sea lion in the Arctic. Winter, as fact and fiction, we're accustomed to conceptualize dangerously. Robert Boldman describes presumed innocence as fraught with fear:

> what happened while we slept   tracks in the snow

There's no knowing. No certitude. No haven. The huge space between "slept" and "tracks" encodes the poem with that which we cannot abide: *aporia.* We are vulnerable, even while we sleep, and sleep is no antidote, as it, too, oftentimes enough leaves "tracks" in the passageways of our minds to places we'd rather not visit. This poem is neither inside or outside; it is both. Treachery; its trajectory. It's shadow.

This is Mr. Boldman's quest, his question. Who am I? By extension, who are we? He gives us a tentative answer in the biographical section of the book at the end.

> i am not good at talking about myself. i used to be...each
> moment is as self-erasing as a dream-an open-ended, wild-eyed
> dream...no seer or seen, sightseeing without a seer.

Indeterminacy (equivocality) best serves in the language game to express this suspension of the self as an entity. Mr. Boldman uses it in the next poem; he posits a self, as a possession, that is "still," while the snow falls; or does he posit that he is, this self is and always was the snow falling?

my self

      still

   snow

       falling

The use of visual/concrete spacing of the words of the poem naturally impacts how the reader understands it: whether intentionally equivocal or not, if "my self" physically resembles in the state described "snow falling," the likeliest interpretation is this self is and continues to be the falling snow itself.

While it may be untrue that there can be a self separate from all other things, and while the tension and fear that accompany our usual way of perceiving ourselves as such is painful, nevertheless the loss of all boundaries between inside and outside is tantamount to terror: before the absence of a self, the individual feels fear, performs supplication, experiences torture, and maybe, just maybe ecstasy. But, it is fraught with dangers. We must be forced to recognize that we are the Void looking at itself, talking to itself, "being" itself, and so we cringe more often than not and step back from the precipice:

mirror   my face   where i left it

Reassurance. I'm intact. The mirror doesn't lie. I am indivisible and there. Just like yesterday and the day before yesterday. Palpable, fleshy, form that will continue on and on. Yet, there is always foreboding. Am "I" a substantive. No. If not, what am I; how do I explain to myself what I am? This non-substantive requires consensus, a socially constructed and construed and agreed upon convention. ("A self does not amount to much, but no self is an island; each exists in a fabric of relations that is now more complex and mobile than ever before. Young or old, man or woman, rich or poor, a person is always located at "nodal points" of specific communication circuits, however tiny these may be. Or better: one is always located at a post through which various kinds of messages pass." (The Postmodern Condition A Report on Knowledge, Jean-Francois Lyotard, 1979). Yet, I am my own absence, darkness, and what I cast is an umbrage, from the Latin *umbra,* a phantom, a ghost; un-real, shadowy (from late 14th Century English, shadewy, transitory, fleeting. Or, where my boundary ends is what I am. As Mr. Boldman writes:

i end in shadow

Robert Boldman ends the first section where it began:

Jan. 1

The corpse of the crow whitens the snow

It's all circular, cyclical, turning and returning. The wheel of life in Tibetan thanka. The beginning is death. Mr. Boldman stresses this paradox by using chiaroscuro (disambiguation) in the strong contrast between Jan. 1, the beginning, juxtaposed to the corpse, the end, and again in the stiff, frozen black of the crow's corpse against the white of the snow. Ordinarily, the effect of chiaroscuro is to highlight the volume and placement of the figure through contrasting shade and light; in Mr. Boldman's poem, the blackness illuminates the whiteness of the less figurative and voluminous snow.

The second section of the book- *not quite reaching*- is a variation on the themes introduced in the first –section- *January First.* While in music, variations on a theme usually refer to a composition by a composer on a theme by another composer, Robert Boldman's variations are incrementally repetitive oscillations, modulations, of his own works, enlarging the scope of the themes as it proceeds.

The first poem is very reminiscent of William Blake's "The Sick Rose":

O Rose thou art sick.

The invisible worm,

That flies in the night

In the howling storm:

Has found out thy bed

Of crimson joy:

And his dark secret love

Does thy life destroy.

Here is Robert Boldman's poem:

beside his sickbed

a rose not quite reaching

the water in the jar

The rose the red blood and its blossoming - a heart - just out of reach of the
evaporated water in the vase; the source of life denied; the person in the sickbed,
soon to lose the ruddiness of life. Death articulated, but "not quite" its moment. We
are drawn in as witnesses, not voyeurs, not sentimentally. The barest essentials of
the death bed. Such a simple matter to alter the arrangement, just a bit more
water or longer stem. Just a little longer to hold on. Compassion is awakened, but
it will not change the outcome.

This vision is Robert Boldman's: the dark journey, the shadowy insubstantial,
even in what is already lifeless, the repetition of death:

day darkens   in the shell

Then again we have another shadow, as the casting of the future, foreshadowing, as
exegesis, as the fleeting and unreal, as enigma, as an association with the
crucifixion, as an example of a cut as the "impossibly true?" (The Disjunctive
Dragonfly, Robert Gilbert, www.iyume.com/dragonfly/DisjunctiveDragonfly.pdf)

the priest

his shadow caught

on a nail

A variation on a theme: a single heartbeat, a synecdoche, the state of the wholly
human in face of the sublime, in its two aspects, as beatific and horrific. Mr.
Boldman creates a temenos, a space reserved for the sacred, for surrender, for us to
assuage the encroachment of our constant fear of death. He uses the word "chapel,"
as this place, which has an interesting etymology. While not denominational, the
word's origin is as the following:

> The word "chapel" is derived from a relic of Saint Martin of Tours:
> traditional stories about Martin relate that while he was still a soldier,
> he cut his military cloak in half to give part to a beggar in need. The
> other half he wore over his shoulders as a "small cape" (Latin: capella).
> The beggar, the stories claim, was Christ in disguise, and Martin
> experienced a conversion of heart, becoming first a monk, then abbot,
> then bishop. This cape came into the possession of the Frankish kings,
> and they kept the relic with them as they did battle. The tent which

kept the cape was called the capella and the priests who said daily Mass in the tent were known as the capellani. From these words we get the names "chapel" and "chaplain". (Wikipedia)

Mr. Boldman's poem:

in

the chapel

a heartbeat

In the remaining poems on the section, Robert Boldman looks on death directly, each poem an examination of an aspect of the human response to the event. In the first, there is a gathering of mourners, that testifies to our intent interest in death, our commemoration of the dead, yet there is a more somber reading possible: the poem may suggest that the gathering is a way to protect us from the coffin in numbers, the sign of finality too much to experience alone, unaided (or, alternatively, the mass gathering could demonstrate the popularity of the deceased). The poem is stark, simple, yet also multi-layered as to meaning:

between mourners

a glimpse of the coffin

The last two poems of this section embody the passage of time. The first does so in an interesting way. Firstly, as it is read, the present passes into the past and then its past disappears, as well. Secondly, the poem was written in the past, so its content, its presence, already marks its past. Thirdly, the poem's subject relates how the death of an individual means the end of a world; it takes the past with it.

the hearse going by

the past

going with it

The final poem of the sequence contains a strange collocation of elements:

suitcase

beside the grave

soft rain

One is tempted to look up the various ways haiku can be disjunctive to parse the poem: it can be seen as imagistic fusion, or metaphoric fusion, or possibly register shift (The Disjunctive Dragonfly, Richard Gilbert, Ibid.). Yet, it doesn't seem to really require such complex textual analysis (though evidently all three types of disjunctive are operating in this field of force). The "suitcase" placed alongside ("beside") the "grave," suggests that death is akin to travel, the great journey. "soft rain" certainly disrupts the two images above it: its purpose, seems similar in kind to the "suitcase" placed by the grave: it is meant to soften the starkness of death, the terror of it, to make it natural, thus not threatening.

In the section *invisible,* Mr. Boldman proceeds with variations on a theme, with new tones, textures, variables, combinations. Yet, there is always an overarching sense of the somber (the shadow) in the poems. Even in a moment of joy:

a day of passing clouds

the heart in my ribs

caged

the poet cannot let go and surrender to the passing pleasure suggested by " a day of passing clouds." While he acknowledges that such an experience tempts his heart to leap outward to greet it, he also remains aware that he/we are "caged," circumscribed, limited. For it is only moment by moment that we live; the transitory is there to cage us. The next poem is minimalist, both beautifully conceived and again limited by the fact that we cannot hold on to anything; it is only a "moment."

a moment   in a box of jade

The extended space between "moment" and "in a box of jade" extends time and space; it makes us pause before the intricate beauty of "jade," so multicolored, soft stone, looking within and finding all sorts of swirls and natural designs in its many greens and white and russet colors. Yet, there is also sorrow here, for it is just a "moment," however you may attempt to stretch it.

In the following three poems, the poignancy of joy/sorrow takes a darker turn (towards the ever-present shadow). The innocence of childhood is taken from us so quickly; the toys we played with replaced, filled-in, by the "newspapers" and there general accounts of the horrors of our world, not to be denied, but recorded, the moments of history black and white tracks of power.

> doll's head
>
> filled with newspaper
>
> clippings

Thoughts replaced, the doll's/child's head forced to absorb "clippings;" even the word "clippings" suggests sharp-edged blades and cutting: we are torn from innocence.

As the philosopher of the famed Frankfurt School, Theodore Adorno, said: "The critique of culture is confronted with the last stage in the dialectic of culture and barbarism: to write a poem after Auschwitz is barbaric, and that corrodes also the knowledge which expresses why it has become impossible to write poetry today." (Prisms, 1955, MIT Press). And Robert Boldman appears aware of the barbaric behind/within culture and history when he presents a poem as a photograph, killing time, "shooting it," as all photographs must, to capture a moment. His poem is pregnant with the future and what is unspeakable about it:

> Death camp in the photograph
>
> the little girl's hair will always be blowing

Such a temptation to arrest time is unavoidable in the context; the poet concentrates on a moment of life, of childhood, of the wind in a girl's hair, and attempts to keep it so forever.

Faced with the terrors of history, it is always tempting to regress, to rewind, to move backwards rather than forward, to a simple "spark," something that suggests light, igniting, but not negatively, not barbarically, rather than depict what explosion and carnage may follow the "spark." Robert Boldman put it this way:

> newsreel rewinding
>
> the terrorist attack
>
> turning into a spark

In the next poem chronologically, Mr. Boldman reintroduces the reader to what is most admirable in culture, turning from the power plays inherent in its construction and maintenance. He uses Beethoven as *representament* of the heights of art, creativity, symphony, harmonics. He places the poem in summer, and by noting the natural and the flats and sharps of the natural sounds of the season, we feel relieved; it is not a sultry night, but a calm, rapturous night. He's taken us back to the Classical and Romantic eras, as far from terrorism and fascism as possible.

> Beethoven: the white keys
>
> & black keys
>
> to a summer's night

And, perhaps by association, we are reminded of Shakespeare and *A Midsummer's Night's Dream.*

The last poem in this section is a bit unexpected, a bit puzzling, insofar as it introduces unexplained categories of language and meaning to the text:

> visible lilacs
>
> shaped by
>
> invisible lilacs

In fact, this poem is perhaps the most "poetic" in the volume, because it takes as its subject the language game (Ludwig Wittgenstein's term for the many different roughly rule-bound language exchanges systems that operate by consensus, not words or sentences themselves. See *The Blue and Brown Books,* Harper, 1958), and intentionally disrupts the consensual meaning of words, thus giving words a non-operational meaning. Equivocation, indecipherability, indeterminacy always accompanies language, but here is an example of the purposeful polysemy of meaning, the meaning behind meaning. Here, one can only conjecture meaning, as there is no definitive meaning to words. Substantives, such as "lilacs" can be named and by social agreement they are shaped into a flower of such and such bush, etc. The word itself, as the linguist Ferdinand de Saussure (*Course in General Linguistics,* published posthumously in 1916) noted, has no natural, motivated relationship to any object. As he said, "Language is no longer regarded as peripheral to our grasp of the world we live in, but as central to it. Words are not mere vocal labels or communicational adjuncts superimposed upon an already given order of things. They are collective products of social interaction, essential instruments through which human beings constitute and articulate their world." (ibid). Perhaps it is this shaping by differential elements socially agreed upon that Mr. Boldman means when he writes of the visible flowers being shaped by "invisible lilacs," or, the formal system of differential elements that language is and is not present/visible to us as we communicate. Wittgenstein (ibid) put it this way: "The sign, the sentence, gets its significance from the system of signs, from the language to which it belongs. Roughly: understanding a sentence means understanding a language." Of course, I assume there are many possible interpretations to be made of Mr. Boldman's poem (supra). I have only suggested one.

In the section *afterimage,* Mr. Boldman offers an interlude. The poems included are quite different from those proceeding and those subsequent. They are lighter. They include muki haiku, that is, haiku without seasonal references; they include haiku that might be called senryu by some. The distinction is not as clear as it has been traditionally presented in the English language world (see Richard Gilbert's Kigo and Seasonal Reference in Haiku: Observations, Anecdotes and a Translation, Publication: Simply Haiku 3.3, Autumn 2005).

The first poem is quite traditional, even with the light-hearted spirit of *haikai:*

> the heat
>
> admiring the shade in the blouse

We have Robert Boldman's referencing shadow (here "shade") once again, but here it is comforting and cool and sensual. It is a humorous use of the unstated, a hallmark in the genre of haiku. It is euphemistic, somewhat like "pillow talk," which reveals Mr. Boldman's knowledge that haiku had its origins in *waka,* an older Japanese poetic form that eventually was referenced, inter-textually in haiku. So, it is actually quite an erudite poem, although its form is decidedly simple.

> in her walk everywhere she's been

This is a compound poem divided between "walk" and "everywhere." The present moment, the movement of the walking woman, reveals all the moments that have led up to the instant time. There's a subtle shift in time being played upon, the language of the body, its entire history, molded in a moment. And, while it might seem a sketch-from-life haiku, we should remember that "her, "she," are not ostensive, cannot be pointed to, so that the poem-intentionally or not-relies on further explanation, which never ends, because it is made up of words that require more words, *ad infinitum.*

> a face   wrapping a champagne glass

The extended space between "face" and "wrapping" creates *aporia*. We do not know, we are not meant to know, whether the face belongs to the person "wrapping," or whether these are fragments meeting, held together loosely. We have here an example of either "the impossibly true," or perhaps "the unsatisfactory object" (Gilbert,noted ibid). A "face" cannot, at least in our common sense of the term, wrap a champagne glass. As synecdoche, maybe it can. But, however it is understood the subject "face" does not ordinarily take "wrapping a champagne glass" as its object. We have irruption of normative understanding in this poem, thus leading to deeper, multiple possibilities of meaning.

lightning

lightening   her kiss

We have the playfulness of homonyms in this poem. Literally, the "lightning" frightens "her" off from her fervency and "lightens" it. Symmetrical rhythmic substitution was the phrase coined by Richard Gilbert (Disjunctive Dragonfly) to describe such word substitutions occurring in symmetrically rhythmic patterns. Two different categories of words appear to be the same and meaning is thus temporarily deferred.

fireworks

taking the afterimage

to bed

Is this poem merely relating a memory so strong and wondrous that the poet retains the original image/light after exposure to it is gone, so much so that he takes it to bed. Afterimages are optical illusions that continue without a source (though they had a source initially). In one sense, this is a summer haiku and an original poetic rendering of how deeply "fireworks" can be experienced. On the other hand, following the poem about a light source, "lightning" and "her kiss," there is an inclination to infer some substitution taking place, some more pillow talk, some sensual experience, a woman perhaps like "fireworks" taken to bed.

I mention this latter reading, because of the context and because the following poem is another relating the sexual experience by proxy:

mist,

panties on the line

116

It took some time before I realized why Robert Boldman did not designate a color for the panties, because that would certainly have highlighted the object in the mist. Then, it occurred to me that, no, the "panties" were like "mist," that is likely sheer or transparently thin. There is something voyeuristic about this poem and so I leave it to the readers' imagination to interpret the preceding poem about "fireworks" and their afterimage taken "to bed."

a cloud

carries away

awareness

The first impression of this poem is that it uses anthropomorphism; the cloud has the quality of a being able to carry away awareness. This is a mythic element in Robert Boldman's work. It disrupts traditional thought and lends an air of the archaic ancestry of poetry to this single poem. On the other hand, the poem can be understood to mean that a "cloud" drifting by is so dreamlike that the poet's "awareness," concentration to thoughts of a real, are simply carried away and he drifts in the sky. There is no judgment here. The poem is, as are the poems in this section of the book, light-hearted.

The penultimate section- *between stars*- returns to the *gravitas* of earlier sections. While season references in haiku may not conform to their attempted equivalence to *kigo* in Japanese haiku (*kigo* are based on a *saijiki*, thus they are literary/seasonal constellations), the first poem in this section seems to draw as near as possible to a legitimate use of *kigo*. Cicadas, so commonplace in our experience of the end of summer or early autumn, while not a subject in our long line of literary heritage, nonetheless evoke an immediate sense of time/space in us. Robert Boldman's poem gives us a unique representation of this often used image in English language haiku:

cicadas   tightening a memory

Following the preceding poem, this poem concentrates the mind that was set adrift. The uniqueness of the poem relies on a reversal of expectations: usually, poems about cicadas reference the outward movement of sound in contrast to a profound surrounding silence. But, Mr. Boldman hears in the sound "memory," and in the shrillness of the cicadas' call a tightening of it, a centering of it. We are drawn inward and to the past. In a sense, the poems reminds me of Gaston Bachelard's *Poetics of Space* (Grossman Publishers, 1969), where Mr. Bachelard describes the connotations and memories invoked by our "idea" of our original home, of the sensorium that arose memory in architectural spaces (the echoes of the past travel through all the corridors).

In the next poem, Robert Boldman returns to an earlier subject, that is, the "subject." In order to allow for other existents, the subject must withdraw, make room for what apparently is other. However, when the subject withdraws, mind, which has no form, illuminates and reflects, realizes its nature in Nature (or whatever it experiences). It is akin to Lévy-Bruhl's *participation mystique,* a state in which a person identifies with objects. In *Man and his Symbols* (Dell Publishing, 1968), Carl Jung described it thus:

> The further we go back into history, the more we see personality disappearing beneath the wrappings of collectivity. And if we go right back to primitive psychology, we find absolutely no trace of the concept of an individual. Instead of individuality we find only collective relationship or what Lévy-Bruhl calls participation mystique (Jung, [1921] 1971: par. 12).

Here is Robert Boldman's poem: (note that the repetition of "utterly" furthers identification of subject/object and relates it by the self-referential nature of language: to "utter," to make a sound, as well as to be complete and whole as an adverb "utterly."

> utterly still
>
> the bluejay cries
>
> utterly what I am

In the following poem, Robert Boldman gives us a poem that Longinus would refer to as the sublime. It is reminiscent of Basho's famous: "The rough sea—extending toward Sado Isle, the Milky Way." Here is Boldman's poem:

> summer solstice-
>
> its   shadow
>
> between stars

We are caught up in the immensity of the universe, the umbra between stars, such unimaginable distances. Yet, for all that, the "summer solstice" is an occasion for celebration throughout the world, the longest day of the year, a sign of rejuvenation to us.

Then we are returned to the minute, with associations though to the light of the sun and stars, where the same emptiness exists just on a different scale. Mr. Boldman's shadow returns again, astronomical or with anthropods.

> firefly
>
> on the   web   lit

Then a return to the cosmic:

> between torn clouds
>
> the fading embers
>
> of Mars

But always with the awareness of death (shadow): that is the "key," that turns as Mr. Boldman's body turns.

> turning in my sleep
>
> the skeleton
>
> key

The last section of the book- *shadows*- picks up where the last poem left off: a deft touch, a connection between poems. From shadows, to skeletons, to bones. That is where the music comes from and leads to:

> lark song
>
> down to
>
> its bones

If you walk long enough and hard enough, you immerse yourself in the world and the world speaks and thinks for you. As Dogen Zenji put it: "The color of the mountains is Buddha's body; the sound of running water is his great speech." Or, as Robert Boldman puts it:

> walking with the river
>
> the water does my thinking

Let us recall the title of the book: ***everything i touch***. What does Robert Boldman not touch. He touches everything and everything is quite palpable and yet as we've seen throughout the text, shadowy, insubstantial. Two sides of one. There is a touching moment in this last section that reveals Mr. Boldman's tenderness and fearlessness, his unflinching eye/heart on the world.

touching my father's ashes

All that's left of he who brought up the poet, touched even as "ashes," dust to dust, touching and emptiness.

Then, there is perhaps Robert Boldman's most renowned poem:

leaves blown into a sentence

Professor Gilbert in his typology of disjunction in haiku referenced this poem under the rubric of *The Unsatisfactory Object* (Disjunctive Dragonfly).

> In Boldman, we can see the outer reality of leaves blowing into a shape, say a line, but to become semantic stretches the sense of subject-object agreement... [this] haiku, through [its] use of unsatisfactory objects, activate intertextual metaphor, a sense of metaphor which is neither in the text nor psychologically reachable as a firm conclusion.

This is one way to look at it. On the other hand, this poem above all others in the collection points to the conundrum of objects and language. As noted (supra), in De Saussure and Wittgenstein, there is no "world" outside of language and language is a game of roughly bounded rules, agreed upon by members of a group, that even at its most transparent always retain traces of equivocality and indefiniteness. It is only as a "transitive verb" that "blown" requires "an object," not in other contexts. Language is our world; it gives it order through context and outside of this there are no "leaves."

Wittgenstein refers to words as bearing family relationships, but never understands them as having a one to one relationship with an object. Indeed, he discusses the very word "leaves," in his *Philosphical Investigations* (http://hermes.arts.cuhk.edu.hk/Philosophy/Wittgenstein/pi/). If we have in mind or draw a "schematic leaf," for instance, how proximate to the real leaf must it be to be understood as the leaf another meant when he used the word. Wittgenstein says:

In such a difficulty always ask yourself: How did we learn the meaning of this word ("good" for instance)? From what sort of examples? in what language-games? Then it will be easier for you to see that the word must have a family of meanings.

And this can be expressed like this: I use the name "N" without a fixed meaning. (But that detracts as little from its usefulness, as it detracts from that of a table that it stands on four legs instead of three and so sometimes wobbles.)

Should it be said that I am using a word whose meaning I don't know, and so am talking nonsense? - -Say what you choose, so long as it does not prevent you from seeing the facts. (And when you see them there is a good deal that you will not say.)

As Lois Shawver, offering commentary on the *Philosphical Investigations* puts it:

When we notice that language is never unambiguous, that is much like the blurred leaf, we might ask "can I use a word [correctly] whose meaning I do not know?" There is a sense in which our understanding of the term is limited. Shall we count this as a case of not-knowing?

The problem is that we can see what is known and what is not-known. Our confusion comes not from not-knowing what the facts are, but rather from the fact that the rule that would determine how we should speak is not definitive enough to tell us how to answer.

So, we end with touching on post-modernist poetics. This is a tribute to Robert Boldman, because it exemplifies his ability to touch everything. His poetics are those of investigation, examination, minimal, unflinching and unsentimental in viewing the world through the medium of language. His is an exemplary and daring poetics that never wavers when faced with the negations, the shadows, cast by the objects/words of the world. He has reconnoitered the labyrinths of his age and found the way out is the way in.

then I must go to the Mountain: (space reserved) for Marlene Mountain

Perhaps, it is a truism to say that reading the works of Marlene Mountain is equivalent to reading the history of haiku in English, but some truisms bear repeating and this one certainly qualifies. There has not been a poet of her stature to emerge in the field since she first started writing haiku in the 1960s and her poetry began with a bang not a whimper or, keeping with T.S. Eliot, her "end is in her beginning." So, I will begin by following the injunction of Eliot's master craftsman, Ezra Pound, who recommended young poets to first read their contemporaries and then read backwards in literary time. I will begin with Marlene Mountain's most recent work that appears in Haiku 21 (Modern Haiku Press, 2011) working backwards or slantwise towards her beginnings. Time doesn't seem so imperative when analyzing Ms. Mountain's work, because from the beginning she was experimenting with the haiku form, never satisfied to fulfill the expectations or demands of the then paradigms set forth by the existing patriarchal order.

Let's have a look at one of the poems in Haiku 21:

out of nowhere isn't

We can possibly make "sense" of this poem by interpreting "out of nowhere" as a non-existent category, an "isn't." However, we can just as well, and this seems more plausible, to consider the poem as an instance of what Richard Gilbert called "dis-completion," that is a poem that disallows completion, "disassembles attempts at reaching a significant coherent meaning-at the same time as meaning is being posed. (Roadrunner Haiku Journal, 11.3). Professor Gilbert considers such poems as codicils of expectation that are thwarted, so much so that the very definition of haiku as a genre is threatened, retreated from. This is Marlene Mountain at her best, but she achieves similarly disassembling even in language games that are more familiar:

a loss of content shapes painted over left to their own design

Is this Ms. Mountain's Kandinsky's Concerning the Spiritual in Art (Dover, 1977)? Content, matter, what matters, what we hold on to for dear life is lost, leaving shapes painted (colors and figures as meaning and structure, composition), and yet they still create a design, only their own, not ours. I can't think of another haiku in the English language that commands such respect for the accidental, the random, operating outside the boundaries of our rules. (Lest it be forgotten, Marlene Mountain is also an artist and has been painting for as long as she has been writing haiku). Here is another poem in a similar vein, where Ms. Mountain leaves things be, doesn't impose meaning where meaning is not (and does so ironically in the medium that most signifies, that by its nature is signifying, that is language):

> left to itself a moon without subtitles

She is not afraid to deprive herself, her reader, with the preparation necessary to understand, to offer the rules, the schema, and this creates dislocation, disorientation:

> along with wind and mud and whatever that means if anything

She demonstrates the post-modernist ability to keep an open text, to achieve what the semiotic philosopher and novelist Umberto Eco required of the poet: "I would define the poetic effect as the capacity that a text displays for continuing to generate different readings, without ever being consumed." (thinkexist.com/quotes/umberto_eco).

And, while she has said of herself that she was always serious, even as a child, she can be self-deprecating while simultaneously referencing her signature (Mountain as related to hills in the below poem), her trace of presence in absence:

> toward old as the hills ungracefully

Let's go back to 1977 (all time is synchronous). Marlene Mountain at that time wrote a haiku that had no content other than the formal requirements of the genre: it was more than a meta-poem, it was a demonstration of the emptiness of the formal in-and-of-itself, an aside to those who were seeking a similitude to the Japanese haiku; Note its 5-7-5 formatting:

> -- ---;
>
> - --- ---
>
> --- --.

(Tweed 6:1 1977)

Here are a few more examples of her enticingly provocative style, her language play with the haiku form, the replacement of words for punctuation marks, and the replacement of words for numerals, all in the service of disengaging the reader from the routine reading of haiku:

Frog semi colon

and more sounds now ellipsis

the night period

(Tweed 5:4 6 1977)

too purfick hikoo:

5; 5

7 7;

5 5

(Tweed 6:1 1977)

five‑seven‑five haik(u)!

five five five five five

seven seven seven sev

five five five five five

(Tweed 6:1 1977; poems cited in "Raw Nervz Haiku," 1995)

Besides experimenting with inherited form, technique, and semantics, Marlene
Mountain was an early practitioner of cut-up in haiku (which William S. Burroughs
used in the 1950s and 60s as alternatives to linear narrative), as well as multi-
media haiku, where she used pictures along with words to convey meaning. She
was also amongst the first to create concrete poems as haiku. Her experiments in
the formalities of the haiku genre long preceded similar strains later engaged in by
other practitioners of the form. Here is one of her cut-ups:

Here is an example of one of her concrete poems:

Here is another cut-up, though it doesn't disturb linearity, but uses mixed media as
an intermediary in meaning:

She often used these pictograms to convey new contexts within which the reader could reimagine the world they inhabited; here is a particularly ingenious use of this technique, returning "words" of nature into a piece of paper designed for completely different purposes (say an application of some kind).

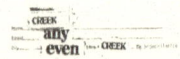

Besides her body of experimental haiku, Marlene Mountain challenged the conventional rule that haiku must contain two juxtaposed images and that no other format was acceptable. She took up the struggle alone to insist that one-image haiku was not only permissible, but was used by the ancient haiku poets. Remember, this argument was advanced in 1978, just as the women's movement was beginning to gain momentum, at the cross-roads of cultural change, and Ms. Mountain took on the male-dominated haiku world alone. It took no small courage to confront the gatekeepers of haiku about what was and was not permitted in the writing of haiku. The essay, "one image haiku," was not only an academic exercise, but marked the turning of an avant- garde poet into a radical, politicized, feminist poet.

It was not merely that Marlene Mountain re-introduced what had always existed in haiku (in Japan), that is, the one-image poem, but that she did so as the "rules" governing the writing of haiku were being consolidated and solidified by a community of writers who had formed a hegemony and dictated to practitioners what was appropriate. To this day, there are some writers of the genre who would insist that anything other than the conventional two-part haiku, one part juxtaposed to the other, is the only viable form for haiku. But, art does not flourish within strictures. Though there is validity to the two image haiku, to require writers to replicate this form in each and every instance is to turn this poetry into the equivalent of following instructions on how to make a paper airplane, or, with some more sophistication, into origami. For those interested in her parsing of modern and ancient examples of the one-image haiku, her essay is available on-line at : (www.marlenemountain.org/essays/essay_oneimage.html)

It was at this juncture in her career as a poet, that the women's movement gained more recognition and pervasive influence in the West, and Marlene Mountain re-created herself as an activist, feminist poet. Much was at stake culturally surrounding the issue- five thousand years of male dominance of societies- and Marlene Mountain gave the strength and talent of her voice to challenge the patriarchal. While some of her poems from this period no doubt might seem polemical, there are more that are simply good poetry, poetry bearing a message. She was not didactic: she was enraged. There are many sources of instances of her feminist writings: one such is an essay entitled "shetrillogy." It is a long narrative essay in which Ms. Mountain creates words to portray the patriarchal view of history up until the present moment and replace it with a new woman-language (1987). There are some marvelous poems included in the essay, poems that speak to the feminine as an equal and balancing valence to the male, as well as some that make of womanhood a "wholeness" unto itself or a shared experience with other women. Here are some samples:

womocreativa

i am no beginning i am no end

i am chaoscoswommos

from my womwomb all is

from my gynitals all flows

birth of wom harvest of wom

shesharing i will make myself into ourselves

sheyes again i will shegive a big birth

Before moving on to further examples of her feminist haiku, it seems important to have a look at a self-interview she conducted in 1982 that was published in "Wind Chimes #6." The work was titled "two femmarks, inner-review," and it explores her views on writing and feminism (and note that she had to divide herself within/without to find a sponsor of the dialogue; the lack of a credible male interviewer speaks volumes to the tone of that time). In fact, the imaginary interviewer questions the validity of Ms. Mountain's haiku in just the way one would expect: that she makes up words, that she emphasizes ideas rather than images, that rather than seek "oneness," so important to earlier practitioners of the art and still considerably important to those writing today, she poses un-oneness. For instance, the imaginary interviewer points out that her word "taliswoman," is not a real word and is an intellectualization. Ms. Mountain answers in a most illuminating way:

> My moment of awareness was that 'talisman' is a concept, a made-up word. Mankind is a made-up word. If you understand that 'man' is not a generic term, but a political idea (that was an overwhelming moment keenly perceived), then the feminization of a word can be a natural response. Or in my case, 'taliswoman' was a hit-on-the-head-with-a- stick. A leap. A breakthrough. Now I'm giving you the word, the leap.

> I: Aren't you asking us to accept an intellectualization?

> M: Not to accept is the intellectualization. In one second the word/moment can become a part of you. Mary Daly, in her discussion of therapist, gives us a word--hits us on the head: the/rapist.1 That's very immediate to me.

> I: She doesn't call that a haiku, does she?

> M: I call mine haiku.

> I: And your definition of haiku?

> M: How 'bout, life?

> I: Is that all?

> M: That's a lot.

Regarding the un-oneness haiku, Marlene Mountain gives us a wrenching example of the common world-wide practice of female castration:

clitoris of the four year old removed

In order to appreciate Ms. Mountain's poems of politics, it is necessary to understand that in retrospect and prospect they were/are radical, that is, further examples of her expansive, experimental writings: they are not to be understood as vagaries of an established normative form. She gives the context within which her poems are to be interpreted in another self-interview: "Innerview" (1981). Here she defines the changes her poetry underwent when she became aware that poetry was always political, that she had previous to her politically engaged poetry simply been naïve. As she said somewhere, "I will not have content taken from me." Here is a sample from "Innerview":

> Though progress has been slow, and repression still abounds, woman has begun to regain some of her rightful rights. The image of woman, however, remains clouded with many many misrepresentations. It is in this light, and for these reasons, that a piece such as Yarrow's--with either a covert or an overt reading--can be effective in establishing a spiritual bond with the past, and in restoring woman's original image.
>
> I: You're throwing haiku into the political realm.
>
> M: It's already there. In an age such as ours, omission is as much political as . . .
>
> I: Haiku is not . . .
>
> M: Haiku can be a lot more than pears and yellow windows.
>
> I: Why do you insist upon stressing the political and the female?
>
> M: I'm not stressing the political, rather, I am recognizing its existence, and within this recognition I am involved in reexamining the direction, potential, and truth of both my painting and haiku. At first, I felt that the potential of painting was wide open and that haiku had many built-in limitations. Now, I've come to see it was my own preconception of haiku that was the limitation. I no longer see haiku as a 'pure' art form, protected from the climate of the times.

Women's Art/Art As Activism. For me now that's all one word. Woman as Protest. Woman as Spiritual. Woman as Physical. Woman as Autonomous. Woman as

Herself, by the very fact of living in a patriarchal world, is Political. And along with that, as She says this and does that, She is an Activist. (1987)

Marlene Mountain wanted to create a new language game, one with new rules (with as little equivocation as possible), without *aporia*, that addressed "identity" in a new way. This is what raises her art above mere didacticism. She has a whole series of what she called "pissed off poems and crosswords," the crosswords being a pun on the everyday play of language game in newspapers and magazines, now cross=angry. She wrote a series of poems under the rubric "late night without mahler" (1985), mahler being referenced perhaps because of his womanizing tendencies and dictatorial conducting manner. In the following poem, we see the objectification of the objectifier:

exhibition of women by male artists

And, in one poem she points to the fact that even language, which seems gender neutral, is not:

thousands of women gather and talk in spite of language

And in "rain a nature sequence," (1985), we can see just one example of why this is so:

ruins the flow of language to correct the sexism

change every he to da see how he da feels

In "i grow older," (1985) she shows us what it is she is challenging:

not against men in general just generals and

autumn nears a gun sale

And, in order to be true, she was daring enough to seem politically incorrect, whereas she was being politically correct: coretta: [10/85]

coretta: he never once mentioned women's oppression

coretta: he never once mentioned women's oppression

coretta: he never once mentioned women's oppression

coretta: he never once mentioned women's oppression

coretta: he never once mentioned women's oppression

Wind Chimes #18; Women and Language

She even created art in conjunction with her haiku that served to illustrate (as in a crossword puzzle) the language of patriarchy:

of females and the opposite of males:

Marlene Mountain also had a vision of God as the alibi of patriarchy and

parochialism: she produced some startling mixed media works to illustrate her views/feelings:

As inventive, as critical, as important as Marlene Mountain's haiku history has been, there have been her detractors: their denial of her work as haiku results from their definition of haiku: the Haiku Society of America formed a committee to define the genre (as if consensus was the method to arrive at truth). For them, haiku is and will always remain "a 'Japanese poem recording the essence of a moment keenly perceived, in which Nature is linked to human nature.'"

Hiroaki Sato, in his essay "Divergences in Haiku"(speech given in 1999 to the HSA) says in this view of haiku, the 'haiku moment,' however defined, is crucial. Sato also stated that as Cor van den Heuvel says with uncharacteristic politeness in the foreword to the third edition of his Haiku Anthology, what Marlene Mountain calls 'pissed off poems,' for example-pieces that 'express her outrage at what we have done and are doing to harm the environment and to limit the freedom of women'-are, 'however admirable, something other than haiku or senryu.'"

Mr. Sato does not take a stand, at least directly, but offers a series of haiku by Ms. Mountain, calls them haiku, which in itself is illuminating, and then says many would not consider them as haiku. Here are the poems in question:

> well, just who the hell do you think fucked it up, caterpillars

> spring in america water unsafe food unsafe sex unsafe

> i'm committed to your maleness even more to the moon's femaleness

> scratched into the mountain shadows of the moon

> a dirty business but someone has to be mother nature

Perhaps, the appraisal of Marlene Mountain that is most important of all comes from Haruo Shirane, author of the influential book Traces of Dreams: Landscape, Cultural Memory, and the Poetry of Bashô (Stanford University Press, 1998): in 2001, he wrote to her:

Dear Marlene,

> I consider Higginson to be a close friend and I admire his work greatly, but here I must offer a different opinion with regard to your work. Whether or not it fits some definition of haiku is of little relevance in the larger picture. The fact is that it is superior poetry, much superior to almost the entire body of what has been narrowly defined in North America as *haiku.* Basho, like his great rival, Saikaku, felt that it was not form that counted, it was the poetry, the quality of the words, how it could move the reader. In their younger years, they broke all kinds of rules. Saikaku was criticized severely, and was told he was just *blowing dust.* But it was in the process of breaking rules

that these poet often made their greatest poetic achievements. Great poets don't stick to rules; they make their own. You belong in that company.

To put it another way, what was most important for Basho was what was called *haikai spirit,.* to be constantly seeking new horizons, new forms, new words, new emotions. (See my book, Traces of Dreams.) In my view, you have that spirit.

Haruo Shirane (Columbia University)

A similar opinion of the work of Marlene Mountain is offered by Professor Richard Gilbert: in his essay titled "A Very Warm Mountain," he introduces the essay with a one of Ms. Mountain's poems:

autumn mist oak leaves left to rust

(Frogpond 26:1)

He says Ms. Mountain has "crafted an oeuvre which offers numerous haiku re-conceptualizations in the *gendai* spirit, an important term from the Japanese haiku tradition meaning 'modern, contemporary.' Mountain offers readers a range of possibilities for presenting contemporary social issues in haiku, and importantly, through her prevalent one-line form, has presented *gendai* re-conceptualizations of the natural in haiku."

He goes on to say of the poem noted supra " The above haiku is one of her more imagistically concrete poems: even the register shift of "rust" coming at the end of the line remains strongly visual. But "rust" creates imagistic irruption and so, naturalistic irruption. Does rust reinforce the sense of season? This is how irruption seems to create a tension, in terms of nature. The uneasiness; rust instead of russet; rust as weathering metal, as technos not geos. Rust is sometimes sharp-edged, ragged, something that gets you cut (so, cutting), infected; the feeling of decay deforms any rising romanticism concerning beauty of the leaves of the autumn oak in mist. It also seems that the irruptive collocation "mist oak" really catalyzes this unease; this language seems to rebel against meaning, forcing us out of the poem, so we lose contact with the natural, with the naturalness of the read-image, read naturally. Then the power of rust (vivid, solid color, substance) throws us back in again, but as garbage, detritus: cast-off or broken. And yes it's the leaves turning, dying, drying out. But we can't quite accept this in a facile way.

"And why is that important — not to believe? Yes, why should we lose our belief in how we habitually find nature? Just perhaps, nature tainted by the consciousness of language is more honest, in a surprising way. Why may this be? It is painful to look at the truth of our contemporary relationship with nature. The field of literary ecocriticism, shared by Le Guin and Mountain, offers us relevant contemplations which directly impend upon haiku. While there are a number of avenues to consider, one that strikes me in relation to Mountain's haiku is that of Bill McKibben, whose 1991 book The End of Nature showed us that human civilization has lost, in our time, is the very idea of nature as something apart, indomitable, pure: the molecules our biosphere have now been altered by human civilization. From global warming and ocean temperature-rise to acid rain and ozone holes, no heretofore natural biome remains unaffected. In another text, The Abstract Wild, Jack Turner shows how the wilds have been converted to managed zones. How can haiku deal with these new truths, concerning relationships between nature and society? Does "pure" nature even exist, except as a romantic concept?

"Contemplating such deformations of nature and the wild, it may be said that at this point in time, naturalistic haiku are highly artificial. And conversely, that there is a strange and rather mysterious naturalness that arises from deformation. James Hillman discusses this in terms of the need for the pathologic in soul-making — it's become very difficult to recover nature through either romantic or naive modes. This is one reason why the realism-inspired shasei representation style of Shiki, which we have been following as a main haiku guideline, is limited. Not irrelevant by any means, but partial.

Questions such as "where is the wild," and "what is nature" must likely be relevant for poets these days, and they are crucial questions for haiku. Coupled with these questions are the polemics of haiku viz nature. It would be ironic indeed, witnessing increasing ecological chaos, to leaf through page-after-page of picaresque juxtapositional haiku scenes of serene contemplation- — some future literature might well ask, "what were those people thinking?" These days, our zeitgeist demands fresh poetic responses to our global predicament. One dimension of Mountain's search has been to artfully seek the wild in haiku, with a rare and unflinching honesty, and in doing so provide approaches that challenge us to reflect honestly upon our time, and the poetic and political relevance of the modern haiku tradition." (Frogpond, 26.1)

Then, we have from the website tempslibres.org the following assessment of Ms. Mountain's life and work:

Haiku as a protest.

A strong speech, committed haiku, far from Zen, but also important essays about a new conception of haiku. A profession of faith to assert her female identity, to tell women sufferings ('a poll'), problems of the world.

A woman on her feet, who talks straight, about Life.

Marlène Mountain, feminist. Impossible to forget.

Such compelling praise of her work, easily over-rides the negative views offered of her life's work. It has been a remarkably diverse, innovative, experimental work from its beginnings to the present. Let's go back to the beginning, as this essay opened with Eliot's her end is in her beginning. The first book Ms. Mountain published was titled <u>the old tin roof</u> (1976). There are some haiku in the volume that already play with language; for instance, the following poem leaves off on a colon thus pointing to nothing, or the unfathomable, as if only an empty space suffices to explain what precedes it:

> the sun
>
> and the mountain
>
> do this:

Or, again, there is a poem with extra spaces between words, emphasizing the nowhere that the buzzard, the scavenger, the bird of ill-omen and carrion, occupies:

> buzzard   nowhere   into   nowhere

Then, she writes a poem that moves backwards:

> backroad summer
>
> in a mountain
>
> follow

She includes a poem with a word missing letters, a visualization of the one word of the poem:

> sn wfl k s

Here is her interesting take on what was then haiku's emphasis on the present moment, but without the pseudo-epiphany; she arranges it as an equation with a understated calculation and remainder:

tonight

less tomorrow

will do

Finally, she includes a portion of language as meaning as a poem: the suffix, meaning action or process, the result of an action or process, something used in an action or process, something related to:

Ing

There is another poem that merits our attention, inasmuch as it repeats a single phrase three times in order to present, concretely, the action of the phrase:

newly plowed field/newly plowed field/newly plowed field

The book also contains some one word poems, such as the following:

furrow

crow

krik'it

In 1986, Marlene Mountain, in an essay, "will I ever get myself explained? (a partial autobiography) speaks to her relationship to haiku as one of attachment, but not an cozy, comfortable attachment. There came a time when she felt haiku was too detached from the real world and human condition. Yet, she felt haiku could accommodate that real world. In her words,

> Have I gone beyond what haiku is--it's particular, perhaps peculiar, view of the world? Its quietness in the middle of a battlefield, its reverence of nature in the middle of irreverence, its simplicity in the middle of chaos? I don't think so. I've merely brought that 'other side' of life into haiku. (Perhaps, I've pushed.) The battlefield, the irreverence, the chaos are a part of us and, therefore (as I've come to see it), are haiku.

Suffice it to say, Marlene Mountain has been and continues to be one of the most restive, experimental, contentious, controversial, and important figures in the world of haiku. She has not slowed down, even in age, as her poems in <u>Haiku 21</u> demonstrate. Her accomplishments-one of the first to experiment in the use of one-line haiku, one of the first to concentrate on concrete/visual haiku, one of the first to use mixed media/collage as an expression of surprising meaning in haiku, one of the first to incorporate the political/gender identity in haiku, the first to question the necessity of a two-image structure in haiku, the first to use empty diagrams or words in place of substantives or numerals to express the mere formalism of haiku, and one of the first to use spacing of words and letters in unusual ways to elicit further meaning than is usually found in haiku. She is, in short, a giant in the field of haiku poetry. Let's end with a somewhat enigmatical poem she wrote, one that exemplifies her sensitivity, her constant human need for association and closeness to others, her ability to invoke *aporia* to expand rather than to retract meaning:

close to someone in the stars white seeps inward

Sunlight on a Different World: The Poetics of Grant Hackett

> *Two dangers never cease threatening*
>
> *the world: order*
> *and disorder*
>
> Paul Valery
> (Analect)

From biographical material I was able to locate, I found out that Grant Hackett is a free-lance indexer. I wondered if developing the skill necessary to choose the essential words from an entire text to use in an index enabled him to select the best words to use in his monostich poems. It seemed reasonable to conclude that his vocation and avocation strengthened one another. Each activity required the distillation of an entire text (be it the world or a book) into their most rudimentary and essential nature. To satisfy my curiosity, I did some reading of what was available on the monostich poem, as that is Grant Hackett's chosen form of expression. While it is not exactly haiku, it bears enough of a relationship to the critical features of haiku to make the effort worthwhile.

I did a bit of research on the subject of the monostich, but couldn't come up with very much. It seems the first modern example of a one-line poem was written by the Russian symbolist, Valery Bryusov and it went like this: "O, cover your pale legs." The poem has an interesting design, I think, because usually the exclamation "O" is found in solemn, earnest poems, whereas here it is followed by a seemingly annoyed observer making a somewhat sententious remark. The reason for this, I believe, was that symbolism as a movement was often confused with decadence as a movement and here the poet is clearly defining the difference. Having read through the poems of Grant Hackett on his website- Monostich Poet-I could not find any instances where he eroticized his poems and so while it may be merely coincidental, Mr. Hackett's work is within the same orbit of Russian symbolism, in regard to the "decadent."

Besides, Bryusov, Guillaume Apollinaire in his "Chantre" (1914) also wrote a monostich poem that went as follows: "Singer" was its title and the poem went "and the single string of the marine trumpets." Marine trumpets are one-stringed instruments that when played with a bow make a noise like a trumpet. One could say that this poem is a meta-poem, inasmuch as it is self-referential or even concrete: Apollinaire is the singer and plays a one-stringed (one-lined) instrument. Again, there is a correspondence in this fact with the poems of Grant Hackett, as they are often self-referential in both senses of the term: that is, his language refers to his personal experience, as well as to itself, to language per se.

Given the paucity of forebears writing in this form, it occurred to me that Mr. Hackett had, in the American vein, struck out into the wilderness alone, as an individualist and his poems, as you will see are if not individual, nothing is. Besides publishing on his website, he only publishes his work occasionally in Roadrunner Haiku Journal and the Lilliput Review. He has not chosen to publish a book. He is a private person and in the American vein is indifferent to fame, as the above facts taken together suggest. While his work is individual, he is not pretentious, but rather democratic, or so it strikes me.

From further research, I discovered that he first became acquainted with the one-line haiku form in 1978 in Haiku selected for Shikishi (published by Ikuta Press) that was distributed by the Haiku Society of America. Mr. Hackett soon after took to writing in the one-line format, although this was not a direct result of the one-line haiku. Rather, there seems to have occurred a rather mystical experience in which he "discovered" his signature double colon:: that he used between sections of the one-line poem and once that happened he has written thousands of monostich poems.

Mr. Hackett did not feel an especial affinity to haiku, hence the hundreds of monostich poems that can be found on his website. Through January of 2008, he wrote dozens of three line poems. On February 4th of 2008, he wrote his first two-line poem:

Black chrysanthemum:

how does your body full of thunder feel

On February 5, he wrote eleven one-line poems, all with the double colon, which has become his signature to this day. It was as if his imagination had opened a door to the imagination with the inexplicable appearance of the double colon. As Mr. Hackett stated in his introduction to some of his poems featured in Roadrunner Haiku Journal (issue 9.1), "The double colon is there to create an unweighted pause. A pause in the breath, a pause in thought. A pause that is different than the weighted or directional relationship our standard punctuation indicates. And that is also different than a hard line break. The two sides of the thought-pause may exist in harmony or in ambiguity. At the moment of the pause there may be peace or there may be tension. The thought-pause is a poetic tool, a poetic device, used poetically."

In that same introduction, Mr. Hackett distinguished what he wrote from reduction : he said his work in one line was rather a distillation. In effect, he does not begin with a mass of words and then remove what he deems unnecessary. Rather, his poems are momentary utterances, a cry, a statement, a moment. Which is not to say they are unedited, or that he refuses changes in syllables, rhymes, rhythms, images; rather, it means that he views his poems as intuitive experiences or apprehensions.

In the same introduction noted supra in which Mr. Hackett offered some of his poems in (Roadrunner (issue 9:1), he named as his influences the early modernist haijin Ippekiro, along with the surrealists Garcia Lorca and Pablo Neruda, as well as the early Robert Bly, who wrote what was called "deep image" poetry, which shared much in common with surrealism. Since then, I understand he has somewhat widened his poetic influences, and yet remain loyal to Lorca, Neruda, and Bly. It is obvious from reading any of his monostich poems that the surrealist mode dominates. It also seems that he adopted surrealism in order to subvert the naturalistic, realistic trend in haiku, as well as in some mainstream poetry and has done so to fulfill what philosophers such as Walter Benjamin and Albert Camus believed was the dominant force inherent in surrealism: unrestricted freedom, freedom of the whole person.

Walter Benjamin put it this way: Since Bakunin, Europe has lacked a radical concept of freedom. The Surrealists have one. They are the first to liquidate the sclerotic liberal-moral-humanistic ideal of freedom, because they are convinced that "freedom, which on this earth can only be bought with a thousand of the hardest sacrifices, must be enjoyed unrestrictedly in its fullness without any kind of pragmatic calculation, as long as it lasts." And this proves to them that "mankind's struggle for liberation in its simplest revolutionary form (which, however, is liberation in every respect), remains the only cause worth serving." (Surrealism: the last snapshot of the European intelligentsia, 1929).

Albert Camus had this to say about surrealism: "The definitive rupture is explained if one considers that Marxism insisted on the submission of the irrational, while the surrealists rose to defend irrationality to the death, Marxism tended toward the conquest of totality, and surrealism, like all spiritual experiences, tended toward unity. Totality can demand the submission of the irrational, if rationalism suffices to conquer the world. But the desire for unity is more demanding. It does not suffice that everything should be rational. It wants above all, the rational and irrational to be reconciled on the same level....for Andre Breton, totality could be only a stage, a necessary stage perhaps, but certainly inadequate, on the way that leads to unity." (Albert Camus, The Rebel: An essay on Man)

Here is one of his poems in concert with the above-quotes:

> I live in a city surrounded by signs:: tangles enough to deepen
> the eyes

In his Innerweavings (transformations of a single poem by interchanges in their word order and emphasis (found in what is parenthetical and what is removed from parenthesis) he revels in the possibilities of truth and the world:

> The spirit of the bell delivers a cry:: I stare into this world
> without peace

> The spirit of the bell delivers a cry (I stare into this world
> without peace)

> The spirit of the bell (I stare into this world) delivers a cry
> (without peace)

Having said this, I would suggest that Mr. Hackett's vision is more personal than political and that he is not necessarily interested in embedding the revolutionary aspect of surrealism (see Breton, et al on this subject) in his poems. There is no evidence to support a reading of his work as intended to break-down societal barriers: his is more of a personal battle to engage his visionary imagination. His interest is in liberating this imagination from stagnation and the prosaic. His goal is the mystery of ontology, the intuitive, the irrational, the inexplicable. His readings in Taoism and Buddhism further attest to this search.

It seems to me that he has chosen surrealism (or it has chosen you) in order to overcome the "lie" inherent in language, the "lie" that Nietzsche spoke of in <u>Truth and Lies in a Nonmoral Sense</u>:

> Every word immediately becomes a concept, inasmuch as it is not
> intended to serve as a reminder of the unique and wholly
> individualized original experience to which it owes its birth, but must

at the same time fit innumerable, more or less similar cases—which means, strictly speaking, never equal—in other words, a lot of unequal cases. Every concept originates through our equating what is unequal.

Surrealism works by language that is never equal to what it speaks of, so, in this sense, it comes closer to the "truth" than what we ordinarily call conventional language. Here are, I think, a couple of examples of what I mean from his poetry:
Out of touch with the world but close to the bone∷ a window for dawn

"A dream":

Was born after time in the branches of night∷ a dream too bright to be seen

I find in his work an undertaking of the problematic of the subject, the privileged "I," that so much thought and writing in post-modernism examines. The question is whether he uses the "I" innocently, naively, or as a matter of a means to focus on the experience of the world/word/poem. I tend to conclude the latter. Here is one example of his awareness that the "I" is not a distinction, in the sense of independence:

Into the action of wind my branches melt   separateness isn't existence

The French post-modernist philosopher Georges Bataille spoke of what he called the "ipse being," and described its and this dilemma as such:

> This ipse-being, itself compound in different parts and as such a result, an unforeseen coincidence, enters the universe with a will to autonomy. It is compound, but still it tries to dominate. Pursued by fear it yields to the desire to subjugate the world under its autonomy. The ipse-being, this minuscule little part, this unforeseen and purely improbable coincidence, is condemned to wanting to be different: to be all/everything and necessary. (....) But this will to being a universe is simply a ridiculous challenge to unknowable infinity. Infinity escapes all knowledge. It escapes always the eyes of a being that is looking for it, by escaping the improbability it is (....). [the Inner Experience p. 118].

Louis Althusser, another post-modernist philosopher, posits the "self," the "subject," as a social construct and not as the independent being within the society:

> In the essay 'Ideological state apparatuses' of 1970 Althusser argues that 'ideology has the function of "constituting" concrete individuals as subjects'.[13] He means that the Subject is an effect of the ideology, not the other way around. Ordinary thinking would have it that persons — Subjects — have ideas, or perhaps more cynically that an ideology is crafted to deceive these Subjects about their true conditions. But Althusser goes further than that. He is saying that ideology does not only deceive you into thinking things like 'this war is a just war', or 'wealthy people worked hard to get where they are'. Althusser argues that even the idea of one as a Subject, author of your own destiny, is an illusion fostered by ideology. ("Postmodernism and the 'Death of the Subject'," by James Heartfield, 2002).

Alongside Mr. Hackett's acknowledgment that separateness is non-existence, there are the threads, the seeming revolt of what could be considered the Romantic Self, the self Bataille said wanted to be everything (as a solution) and this is something that needs scrutiny. Here are Mr. Hackett's poems:

> When the last sound comes I will call to myself   there's nobody but you in the world

> When form wears out and soul is consumed   how will I chew upon the bones

But writing, in the post-modern terminology, doesn't have an author. Roland Barthes, another French philosopher, put it this way (and this also speaks to Mr. Hackett's poems about "origins," which I will quote momentarily).

> "Linguistically, "Barthes declared, "the author is never more than the instance writing, just as I is nothing other than the instance saying I: language knows a 'subject', not a 'person'." And he famously concludes: We know now that a text is not a line of words releasing a single 'theological' meaning (the message of the Author-God). . . . The text is a tissue of quotations drawn from the innumerable centres of culture. The writer can only imitate a gesture that is always anterior, never original. His only power is to mix writings, to counter the ones with the others. . . . Succeeding the Author, the scriptor no longer bears within him passions, humours, feelings, impressions, but rather this immense

dictionary from which he draws a writing that can know no halt: life never does more than imitate the book, and the book itself is only a tissue of signs, an imitation that is lost, infinitely deferred. (Cited in "Language Poetry and the Lyric Subject," by Marjorie Perloff, 1998, internet site).

Or, as a member of the Language School, Lyn Hejinian put it:

--The "personal" is already a plural condition. Perhaps one feels that it is located somewhere within, somewhere inside the body--in the stomach? the chest? the genitals? the throat? the head? One can look for it and already one is not oneself, one is several, incomplete, and subject to dispersal. ("The Person and Description," Poetics Journal 9, 1991).

He also has a number of poems that mention "origin," and yet "origin" is itself a problematic, because it is a matter of who constitutes that origin, what power props it up. Here are his poems:

A closed sky opens:: the lost sun shines:: I live to obey my beginning

The sound of singing in a darkened sky:: self spills from silence to source

In his poetry, though, there is a sensuality of death, something of a longing for death, and here I think he joins with Georges Bataille's mysticism, and finds his resolution for the illusory self-existent.

The pull of all existence is towards the sacred. In the sacred the original and natural communion of all being is felt to be present without alloy. Life wants to merge into life, because it intuits its own transtemporal unity. This unity it finds again in the sacred. So what I want as an individual and what we want as a global community is the same thing: our heart yearns for the sacred. We want the suspension of the ipse-being in the communion the sacred re-enacts. (Georges Bataille, www.mysticism.nl).

So, we have some of his remarkable monostich poems that are death and not death, communion finally:

Returning to the sky (time will change color) to endure without dying (rain will take my shape)

The moon climbs from a place out of reach:: my midnight within
and waiting

Prior to the moment walls fell away:: moonlight accepted my
name

Into the garden I pour my stillness:: will have the whole sun
after death

The decay of day promises beauty:: we stop to take the dying in

Stars go out that guide my life:: I dissolve in the current I seek

The difference between Grant Hackett's vision of communion and Bataille's is
that Mr. Hackett proposes it without fear, torture, supplication, and yet most
importantly he does not advance a plan; there is no pretense of knowing, no
intellectual categories of the infinite that finally kill it off. And that, I think, is
wherein Mr. Hackett achieves the goal of over-coming the indulgence and delusion
of an independent and privileged self in his poetry.

From my perspective, Grant Hackett uses surrealism in a way that conforms
to what the Russian philosopher Mikhail Bakunin had in mind when he said "the
passion for destruction is a creative passion." (1842). What I mean is that rather
than enclose meaning his poems open meaning to multiple renderings, to polysemy.
His poems do not use the written text in order to deceive, to create
authoritarianism. He does not suppose that the word is made flesh, that once the
code of his poems is interpreted, the scales of flesh fall off only to leave the
resplendence of *a* meaning. Here is one I love that suggests not only a similarity
between stars and jasmine blossoms, but simultaneously there is a suggestion of the
self as the other:

The other voice could be talking with stars:: winter jasmine

Another example of a poem in which he signals the expansiveness of the
world and the puissance of the "light" of knowledge, of consciousness, of love (it's
indeterminate, as it should be) to compose it, to keep the world from becoming an
overwhelming materiality and sensorium, is the following:

Like a dark love singing through thousands of mists:: I knew I
held moonlight inside

Then, there is a marvelous poem he wrote that relies on role reversals of a
kind, where contrary to readers' expectations that they are the center of the

145

universe, interpreters of it, the vast, cosmic ocean, of which we are composed, perhaps an origin or not, reads us and not the other way around. The overturning of roles forces the reader to participate in the completion of the poem's "meaning" and this is precisely what an *open* poem does: rejects closure:

> Though I will never feel the cold salt waves:: all my life I am
> read by the sea

In one of his poems, he explicitly denies the possibility of closure, of a final destination or interpretation to the world:

> A sun comes up where no sun existed:: that morning is not to be
solved

> To put this process initially into perspective, I offer the following analysis:

> I can only begin a posteriori, by perceiving the world as vast and over-whelming: each moment stands under an enormous vertical and horizontal pressure of information, potent with ambiguity, meaning-full, unfixed, and certainly incomplete. What saves this from becoming a vast undifferentiated mass of data and situation is one's ability to make distinctions. The open text is one which both acknowledges the vastness of the world and is formally differentiating. It is form that provides an opening.

> Lyn Hejinian (cited in The Rejection of
Closure.doc, 1983,   (Given as a talk given at 544
Natoma Street, San Francisco)

When he composes a poem he is aware of the dilemma positioned in language to both seek order and disorder, or un-boundedness and containment of the forces it sets in motion.

In what he calls his Innerweavings, where he writes variations of a "single" poem, we can find his awareness of the various tensions, impulses, forces working through the creation of one form in distinction from another: he achieves an open text in this manner and does so in a most laudable fashion.

> Shoulder to shoulder life works my soil:: in a place out of reach I
am waiting

> Shoulder to shoulder life works my soil (in a place out of reach I
> am waiting)

146

> Shoulder to shoulder (in a place out of reach) life works my soil
> (I am waiting)

I think we see here once again of what Lyn Hejinian had in mind in her remarks in "The Rejection of Closure" (Ibid).

> Writing's forms are not merely shapes but forces, formal questions are about dynamics- they ask how, where, and why the writing moves, what are the types, di-rections, number, and velocities of a work's motion. The mate-rial aporia objectifies the poem in the context of ideas and of lan-guage itself.

Then, again there is role reversal, indeterminacy, where an "object" of beauty gives itself away completely to one who receives it, but in an unexpected way:

> The pearl that loves you will have forgotten its beauty:: a light
> no one sees

Or, where he literalizes the metaphoric, thus creating a "gap" in understanding, giving the reader their right to labor, freeing their labor to interpret, thereby stepping outside of the role as the author as authority:

> Prior to the moment walls fell away:: moonlight accepted my
name

Sometimes, he uses "synesthesia" to prepare the reader to accept the impossible, the surreal, which in its way is more "real" than what we ordinarily refer to as "real":

> Come climb inside the hay-scented sun:: and rocks will sing
when you're old

Occasionally, I find that he creates a confusion of categories, until the ordinary becomes the extraordinary and rather than insist on denotative meaning he allows a "gap" to exist between image and meaning and permits the reader the freedom to relax their resistance to the fashioning of a new world, a new way of perceiving and experiencing the world:

> Day by day:: as the frozen earth walks:: my seasons float with
the world

Amongst the examples Lyn Hejinian gives of the open text is whether form "makes the primary chaos (the raw material, the unorganized impulse and in-formation, the uncertainty, incompleteness, vastness) articulate without depriving it of its capacious vitality, its generative power? Can form go even further and generate that potency, opening uncertainty to curiosity, incompleteness to speculation, and turning vastness into plenitude? ...Form is not a fixture but an activity." (Ibid).

Oddly, I think we can compare the above-description of an open text to what Mr. Hackett's forebear, Garcia Lorca, called *duende:* in his <u>In Search of Duende</u> (New Directions, 1998), Lorca writes:

> "The duende's arrival always means a radical change in forms. It brings to old planes unknown feelings of freshness, with the quality of something newly created, like a miracle, and it produces an almost religious enthusiasm." [...] "All arts are capable of duende, but where it finds greatest range, naturally, is in music, dance, and spoken poetry, for these arts require a living body to interpret them, being forms that are born, die, and open their contours against an exact present."

We can feel this this power, this evocation in the genuine sound, vitality, imagery Grant Hackett's monostich:

> A pile of dust becomes the sun:: I build my life from life restored

> The colors of sunset last many years:: I read starlight through my walls

> What comes next will always disappear:: the moon turns to dust on my path

> Empty steps are easily ignored:: but moonlight I can use without rules

Sometimes, his use of surrealism, of attribution of qualities that reason cannot fathom, gives his work a depth and imaginative leap that restores us to our "senses":

> The sky you awakened in the eyes of the rain:: holds the moon the night and the reason to remain

I find a subtle expression of the magical quality of a life lived in his work that captures the fleeting moment and his gratitude for it most tender. He says:

> My life is that glimpse of the sky you have as it chases a small bird into breath

Or,

Let wild seed wake:: before the rains turn old: before the moon is shut out of your heart

Though he is not technically a writer of haiku, he has a keen sense of the seasonality of human nature, its reciprocity with environment:

I see the window turning white

before the coming of the snow—

our lives repeat the cold

Or, here:

My soul has shared growing old in a tree:: until each is an accomplice:: in the other's art

Ludwig Wittgenstein opened his famous <u>Blue and Brown Books</u> with the following statement:

What is the meaning of a word?

Let us attack this question by asking, first, what is an explanation of the meaning of a word; what does the explanation of a word look like?

The way this question helps us is analogous to the way the question "how do we measure a length?" helps us to understand

the problem "what is length?"

The questions "What is length?", What is meaning?", "What is the number one?" etc., produce in us a mental cramp. We feel that we can't point to anything to reply to them and yet ought to point to something. (We are up against one of the great sources of philosophical bewilderment: a substantive makes us look for a thing that corresponds to it.) (Harper, 1958)

Ultimately, all that language deals with is not ostensive; more, especially in poetry, where the play of language is flaunted, emphasized, we can situate the work of Grant Hackett; he engages in language games, as do all poets, and the complexities, seeming inconsistencies, conundrums are solved by the context, the knowing of the rules of the particular game being played. Mr. Hackett's poetry is a surrender to the imaginary, to the inexplicable and mysteriousness of being and existence, both open to interpretation and ordered in unique and individual ways. Let me end there with some more samples of his work, as it speaks more eloquently than I ever could:

> If my day's not meant to last :: that first attached me to disorder

> The breath I am shall awaken the winds :: then the last sound comes
this way

> The eyes of my black fires speak from darkness :: eternity has never
asked for light

Typology & Poetry: Richard Gilbert Experiments

Richard Gilbert, currently Associate Professor of British and American Literature, Faculty of Letters, at Kumamoto University since 2002, is perhaps best known for his book Poems of Consciousness, (Redmoon Press, 2008), a book that articulated for English language haiku poets what it was that their poetry was doing, how they worked. Over the course of the past fifty years, rules and boundaries abounded in the form based on whatever was available in translations of Japanese writers on the subject; English language poets selected what seemed germane or useful in writing, but this actually amounted to fragments of knowledge gathered over time; eventually these rules hardened into prohibitions, proscriptions, restrictions that limited the poets' fields of vision; they stopped looking beyond what they had defined and formed from fragments gleaned from the Japanese. With each new publication of a book on the subject translated from Japanese, some new trends appeared in the English form, but for the most part imitation was most esteemed; creativity, uniqueness questioned, more often than not rejected.

With the publication of Poems of Consciousness, all that changed. There were books previously published that paved the way for Poems of Consciousness. Traces of Dreams by Professor Haruo Shirane was one such book, as it introduced the modern linguistic model of diachronic and synchronic axes of coordinates in haiku (that always existed in Japan and was missing in its English relative, leaving the English poems flat, ahistorical, not complex enough to generate a literary criticism). Then, there was the earlier edition of Japanese Haiku 2001 (edited by the Modern Haiku Association [Gendai Haiku Kyokai]). With introductory essays and samples of modernist haiku poets and their works, English language haiku poets had the opportunity to see that haiku in Japan had undergone historical processes in the 20th Century not un-akin to what had transpired in mainstream Western poetry in the 20th Century. For most, this book was a watershed moment for modern haiku in English.

Richard Gilbert was already known to English language haiku poets by his academic and researched essay: "Stalking the Wild Onji," an essay that explained to

Westerners the distinction between sound units (onji in Japanese) and syllables in English, so that the often mistaken idea that haiku in English should be written in three lines of 5-7-5 syllables was deemed invalid.

In Poems of Consciousness, Professor Gilbert combined a number of earlier essays, including the seminal "Disjunctive Dragonfly" (Publication: Studies in English Language and Literature 47, Kumamoto University, Kumamoto, Japan (March 2004), along with translations of modern Japanese gendai poets. He offered a typology of types of haiku disjunction (a term he used in place of what had preceded it historically in defining haiku, that is, juxtaposition or super-position of images), and though not meant as an exhaustive study, it so replenished the vocabulary and understanding of how haiku actually worked as to have changed English language haiku forever.

Professor Gilbert well understood that there was work that remained to be done in defining methods of writing haiku. Just recently in the blog at Roadrunner Haiku Journal, Gilbert introduced a new term for haiku: dis-completion, where a poem is written in such a way it disallows completion, disassembles attempts at reaching a significant coherent meaning.

And, it is here that I wish to start. As John Cage said "Where does beauty begin? Where does it end? Where it ends is where the artist begins." And, so it is with definitions, typologies (however encyclopedic) and poetry. I recently asked Professor Gilbert about his own sparse output of engaging and complex haiku. He explained to me that he wrote poems/haiku "most often ... when ideas relating to a new approach or way to explore the possible range of haiku coalesce." Let's begin in 2004, as that is the date from which the first haiku of Richard Gilbert is available.

dedicated to the moon

I rise

without a decent alibi

(NOON, 2004, Tokyo)

The first line confirms what we would expect in our post-modernist age, that is, the unexpected is placed squarely in the poetic; aporia is embedded in language and poetry takes equivocation of meaning as its topos: is the first line a dedication, as in a consecration, avowal to a person or (in this case a celestial sphere) as in the dedicatory of a book (in miniature). Or, is it devotion, from the Latin devotus, to give oneself away assiduously, in a vow to the moon? Is the moon the narrator's solitary goal, an orbiting rock, satellite, that is dedicated in an equivalent manner to the earth in orbiting it without ever rotating, always facing it? Or is it because they share the linguistic category of "rise?" "I rise," says the narrator; the "moon" we say "rises." They are coequals, co-equivalents. They both have no meaning as a given; both are bodies in time/space; both travel daily, nightly. Without a creator, without something transcending the structure that sets it in motion and to which everything refers for meaning, an alibi, it is hardly far-fetched to equate " I" to the "moon" as both lack a "decent" alibi. There isn't even a crime committed that requires an alibi. The narrator does not have to explain his whereabouts at a given time, because he "exists, just as it can be said that the moon "exists," and it is no crime to exist.

Or, contrariwise, can we say there is something suspicious going on, rising perhaps in the night (time is not specified, only hinted at by the evidence of the moon), that even evokes the need for the word "alibi?" Was he sleeping and he arose? Or, did he just "rise" from a prone position?

Was his action voluntary? Can we say we know or he knows how he rises? Does this include the awareness of the physiology of rising, as part and parcel of knowing what we communicate when we write or speak of rising?

If you look at the typology of disjunctives found in haiku in "The Disjunctive Dragonfly" (Ibid), you will not find a category for the issues raised in this poem; hence, its production and its existence as a possible project for future discourse.

Let's have a look at another poem Richard Gilbert wrote in 2004:

a drowning man

pulled into violet worlds

grasping hydrangea

(NOON, 2004)

A man being swallowed by water (ironically the word stems from the Goth. dragkjan "to give to drink") as in drenched, but "violet worlds" is not our customary way of viewing death by drowning. We may think of "violent" here and I misread the poem the first time based upon expectations of the word that I presumed would follow upon the initial image. But violet reminds us of the beautiful blue/purple of the flower, and hydrangeas, as well. Oddly enough, etymologically the amethyst, a violet quartz, derives from the Greek amethystos "amethyst," lit. "not intoxicating from a- "not" + methyskein "make drunk," from methys "wine" (see mead (1); based on the stone's ancient reputation for preventing drunkenness. So, we have something of a contradiction in "drowning" being related to being drenched, drunk, swallowed in water, and it opposite "violet," related to preventing drunkenness, preventing being drenched, drowned. And, what are the violet "worlds?" Is the drowning place plural, as in underwater "worlds," in contradistinction to "world." In "grasping hydrangea," perhaps we have an answer: the man is not drowning literally, but losing his sense of self in "grasping" (trying to deeply understand) the violet worlds of "hydrangea." Is it the drowning or intoxication of the lineage of Li Po and Du Fu, where these mountain poets used intoxication (drowning) as a substitute for illumination, being de-ranged, experiencing the loss of boundaries between the ten thousand things and the poets. Literally, a drowning man cannot grasp "hydrangea," because they do not grow by bodies of water and they are not so deeply rooted as to save by holding on to them.

Again, we have indeterminacy as central to the poem, as it is to language generally.

Let's have a look at some poems Richard Gilbert wrote in 2008.

after the rush

the hollow sound

of the holy

(NOON, 2008)

We like to think, for security, that words such as "after" have a meaning understood between a speaker/listener or writer/reader; but that is not the case. "After" can be any time and dependent on "before," which is also an indeterminate time. We are not located in time in this poem. Nor does the word "rush" convey a particular meaning. The word is derived from Latin impetus "attack, assault, onset, impulse, violence, vigor, force, passion." Or is its meaning hurdling, rapid? Sometime after one of the meanings of "rush," (perhaps Newton's centripetal: center seeking) we have "the hollow sound" of the "holy." And hollow can be a cave, cavern, a hole, or perhaps from the Old English deop meaning "profound, awful, mysterious; serious, solemn; deepness, depth." The holy is not a substantive; it cannot be pointed to. Indeed, it is quite the opposite, and so it requires usually a sense of "emptiness," and yet needs further words and explanations to interpret it that ultimately have no terminus: it is not a presence, let alone a fully present. Yet, it is only the "rush" that allows its opposite "hollowness" and "holiness" to be thought (if not explained, except through ad infinitum usages of other words).

Let's look at another poem from 2008:

hungover - ignoble

Jerusalem - cactus

pissing   - the cats

(Roadrunner, 2008)

Is this poem exemplary of metonymy? That is to say, is the contiguity of association of divergent things the operative method of the poem? Or is it words that merely by physical proximity and lineation create a sense of unity where there is none? What of the dash between each word in each line: is this a cutting device used in haiku so often? The en dash can also be used to contrast values, or illustrate a relationship between two things. Certainly, we experience a relationship between being hungover as a moral equivalent of "ignoble." Then, we may associate "ignoble" with the holy land, "Jerusalem," as its antithesis. But, if we continue in this vein, we arrive at cactus, a substantive, associatively related to Jerusalem because of its dry, desert-like lands. We have crossed over categories, though, from the judgmental to the physical, unless we understand "cactus," as prickly and thus as a means to punish the profligate with punctures by the needles of cactus. Then, we move to "pissing," which relates to being "hungover," inasmuch as the drinker may still be saturated with liquor/liquid and drunkenness is often associated with "pissing." But what about the association to "the cats?" Are we to understand that one who is ignobly hungover, pissing, descends to the animal level, is no more moral than a "cat?" Perhaps, Or, perhaps the only force holding the poem together is the associations, connotations, renderings of each individual reader and is not meant at all to have a final meaning.

Here is another poem from Roadrunner in 2008:

                    waning gibbous

the increasing density

of fall

The waning gibbous moon often initiates a rash of questions about seeing the moon during the day. If it rises late at night, you know the waning gibbous moon must set after sunrise. In fact, in the few days after full moon, you'll often see the waning gibbous moon in the west in early morning, floating against the pale blue sky. And, as the full moon enters this waning phase, so too does the "increasing density" of autumn begin to wane what is in nature, the leaves, the undergrowth, all the living green. What is interesting in this poem is the semantic disjunction between increasing density with waning moon and fall (the density of which is a lack of density, the loss or fall of nature).

Another from Roadrunner in 2008:

returning bones

a stone unwinds

in the breeze

We have two contrary movements in this poem: centripetal and centrifugal. We have the centering to "bones," a "returning," that seems to imply a resumption of life in the body (perhaps in spring) and the "unwinding" of a "stone," the outward spinning of what had been condensed (perhaps in winter); the conjectures are all based upon "the breeze," suggestive of gentle weather, of springtime. Of course, this rendering of the poem perhaps oversimplifies it. The phrase "returning bones" is itself quite perplexing, another example of poetry as highlighting aporia as its central purpose; its playing with the deficiencies of language as its starting and ending point. The same can obviously be said about the phrase "a stone unwinds," as this is literally impossible. We could call this, as maybe Richard Gilbert would say, an example of the impossibly true disjunction in haiku, a means whereby the metaphoric takes upon itself the burden of meaning and transports the reader to an understanding of the real beyond the ordinary categories within which they understand the real; it is meant to be disorienting, indecipherable, a mystery; it brings us back to the impossibility of the definite.

Let's look at an intriguing poem written in 2010 and published in Roadrunner:

When you dream the inside

smoke between cypress trees

When we dream we think of it as being "inside," somewhere; Frederic Nietzsche went so far as to say that it was because of dreams that the idea of a soul was first imagined my humans. Here, the poem seems to have a number of enjambments. It could very well mean "the inside smoke" lies between" cypress trees. Cypress trees are often associated with flame-like trees that bear relations to death. Perhaps, that is what Prof. Gilbert had in mind when he referred to the "smoke between" these trees. Cypress trees have a long association with the spiritual, with "the inside smoke."

The Etruscans were fascinated by the evergreen nature of the cypress, retaining its leaves when all other trees were bare. They believed the tree had supernatural connections and put the plant around their graveyards. The cypress wood is quite resinous and strong in highly fragrant essential oils. These properties cause it to decompose very slowly, making it an ideal wood for coffins and sarcophagi. The Persian, Syrians and Turks all used the cypress for coffins and the trees were historically planted at both the head and foot of Muslim graves. 44(What Is a Cypress Tree? | eHow.com). Perhaps the poem implies that within, "inside" when you "dream," you are proximate to the spiritual, the "smoke" in the space between these otherworldly trees (that decompose slowly and retain leaves throughout the year, equivalent to a lifetime).

Then there are a number of poems Prof. Gilbert published in 2011 in Roadrunner:

there in the trees to begin with just before and just after

love

This is a poem that thrives on the essentially poetic: where you would anticipate "to begin" to begin the poem, it is placed elsewhere, after a phrase that points to nothing particular- "trees" being a class of kinds, not individuals- and "there" and "in" being equivocality, placement without being knowable. As to "just before" and "just after," we are again, though this time in "time" not "space" placed in uncertainty, indeterminacy, in the play of language, of signifiers that lead to further signifiers but never to a referent, a thing, place, time. And "love?" Well, "love" is a substantive, although it is always different, although it is always moving, never static, multiple physical movements we have no knowledge of, so that if asked do you know what, how you make "love," you really couldn't say for sure, but by social convention you would probably answer affirmatively. So, Richard Gilbert has written a poem of say the Mysterium Coniunctionis, the opposites in alchemy, in Adam and Eve, in the mysterious conjunction of binaries, the Unis Mundus.

Another brilliant poem from the X.1 issue of Roadrunner:

as an and you and you and you alone in the sea

How deftly Prof. Gilbert slowly builds, adds, one letter from "as" "an" to arrive at "and," which linguistically is nothing more than and, additionally, addition, from "an." He is playing with the particles of language. And then what does he do? Why he keeps adding, which is "and," to "you." And "you and you and you." And, most ironically, this you, a pronoun of the second person singular, a mere semantic creation in the language game, the field of language, without "real" substance, adding an and and and still coming up with an "abstraction." For all that this multiple meaning "you," who has no static existence, but is a trace of all the different allusions, memories, others, technologies, sounds, environs, words, and who in time is unfinished and has no control over who they will be and what further influences and interconnections, intertextualities will pass through them and in them, is alone in the "sea" of sensorium. For all that this "you" is anyone in general.

Let's have one last look at Richard Gilbert, poet.

moon cradled you recall the voice of another I might be the distance

This poem virtually rings with polysemy. "moon cradled," may refer to the moon as a cradle in the sky, the clouds as pillows, blankets, as it is in Irish lullabies. Whoever is such in the poem is comforted and they either "recall the voice of another" or "recall the voice of another I," it is impossible to say for sure how the pauses are meant to be taken. Probably, for the sake of multiple meanings the arrangements of the words intentionally leads to polysemy. If the "you" hears the "voice of another I," then that might be the cause of the distance that is existing between them. If, on the other hand, the "you" recalls in memory the voice of another, the narrator "I" might be the distance the "you" travels from the present to the past of another ("I" might be the conduit for the travel across time; "I" might remind you of or call you to "another). We are virtually in frisson. We cannot get out. We both deplore uncertainty and willingly embrace it as our fate in language, in our world of language, in our world wholly mediated by language.

As a literary critic, Richard Gilbert creates typologies of kinds of haiku by gathering together from the whole field examples of poems that work enough in similar ways to deserve to be classified together. As a poet, however, he does the opposite. He leads with what is most relevant to poetry and that is the indeterminacy, the constantly shifting meanings implicit in language. The critical voice is certain, strong, coalescing. The poet's voice is also strong, but it decenters meaning, works by the decentering that already exists in language. It is a meaningful life Prof. Gilbert lives without finality of meaning. That is why we appreciate him; his life is ours.

Descant: Dimitar Anakiev's *Rustic*

In *Red Dragonfly's* blog about the recent (2011) Haiku North America Conference, tucked away in the many accounts of speeches and occurrences was one item that struck me as too important to be treated as something of an anomaly, an addendum: the speech delivered by Dimitar Anakiev, co-founder of the World Haiku Association, internationally renowned film-maker, poet, and erstwhile medical doctor. The speech was directed at what can only be called the new specter haunting Western Europe and the Anglo-American world: that is, the specter of global capitalism and its entrenchment into the deepest and most private spheres of existence (even in so seemingly innocuous a poetic form as haiku).

Dr. Anakiev expressed ambivalent feelings about this state of affairs, since by its nature, haiku was an art form that should of necessity fulfill the human need for inter-relationship with nature and not serve the domination of western materialism.

Here is a portion of Dr. Anakiev's speech:

The "capitalistic haiku" has spread and taken root in its numerous mutations often expressing the spirit which has broken its vitality and uses it as a form without any ontological substance. Such, "capitalistic," haiku cannot be made by any further formal regulations into a "real" haiku, simply because it is not real, or is not real enough, and perhaps is even 'unreal.' Having criticized the "naiveté" of the New Age rebellion against its own culture and having succeeded to adapt haiku from the subculture to the demands of the mainstream, we have to confront with the result and the result is the "capitalistic haiku."

If we ask ourselves what the characteristics of the "capitalistic haiku" are, then we shall notice the maximal reduction of its human content, so that when reading poems of current "capitalistic haikuists" we cannot learn almost anything about their authors as human beings – the whole spectrum of human topics has disappeared and, in the "capitalistic haiku," are dominated by dehumanized topics of nature. Thus, for them, nature is a mere object as if an aim in itself whereas man is most often present as an affirmative witness, and haiku is a record in "index afirmatorum." The need to express something is not noticed; it is replaced by the need for recording. A deeper association is absent, that which is essential to haiku. I guess the so-called "ecological haiku" viewed in this way can be a subtype of the "capitalistic haiku" because a real, essential, connection with nature is replaced by critical conscience. It is doubtful whether "capitalistic haiku "can be considered to be poetry, and it is also doubtful whether it is haiku at all. If it is, it is of the most trivial sort.

We recognize in this description the many haiku that are sketches from life (sashei), where a scene from nature, devoid of human presence, is given to evoke a mood, an emotion by the mere panoply of words on the page. Whether the haiku represents nature as adornment or wholly other, such haiku do sever human and nature as binary opposites.

Karsten Fischer, of Humboldt University, Berlin, in an essay (Journal for Cultural and Religious Theory vol. 6 no. 2, 2005) invokes Frankfurt School Philosopher Theodore Adorno to suggest that

The domination of man's natural environment made possible by controlling man's inner nature leads to a limitation of the human horizon to self-preservation and power. In addition, the justifying idea of a divine commandment to subdue the earth and to have dominion over all creatures reduces the sensitivity of civilized humans for the conditions of their violent domination of nature organized in and by society. Finally, the internalized violent domination of nature also facilitates the use of force in social life. Adorno's hypothesis with regard to a psychology of civilization means that man's brute force against nature encourages him to use violence against other human beings as well.

Of course, following the history of neo-Marxism (which did not separate man from nature, but rather saw nature as the inorganic body of man), we arrive at Jean Baudrillard's hyper-reality, where all members of a society desire possession of the *signs*, the codes, of social hierarchy, so that there is no substance ontology any longer. The label, the name, the brand is all-important and this hunger so saturates the drives of the modern human psyche that human beings can no longer distinguish what is real from what is reified. The very fiber of the psyche is subjugated to appropriation of signs of belonging. As an example of this unconsciousness, the loss of a sense of belonging to nature, and the positioning of the modern "subject," Dr. Anakiev's poem that follows expresses it perfectly:

mall people!

do you know how soon

we will die? (this poem is not included in *Rustic*)

As Karsten Fischer noted (Ibid, supra):

The running wild of self-preservation as a regression of civilization into its former state and antithesis rather results from its ideological justification. This justification demonizes nature and therefore enables its unrestrained, exterminating domination. Adorno does not criticize the domination of nature as such but rather its boundlessness, which leads to its dialectical set-back. This set-back is a dialectical one because, according to Adorno, the absolute domination of nature provokes destructive socio-cultural phenomena, since the domination of fellow humans and the domination of nature are closely related through history in a disastrous way. They cannot be separated from each other.

Hence, we have Dr. Anakiev's poem that stamps on our psyche the savagery that in dominating nature and man in the central act of civilization results in the savagery directed towards other human beings:

Neanderthal man

is bombing Afghanistan back

to the Stone Age

Here are Dr. Anakiev's remarks on the poem:

The idea for this poem came after the first massive bombings of Afghanistan in 2001. It was published on the Italian poetry site Casa della Poesia as a part of their "anti-war" poetic action. Apart from this poetic event it has less in common with any particular criticism than with speaking about the very nature of mankind: humanity is continually enacting a modern Stone Age, without any ability for moral progress.

And democracy is no guarantee against the ferocity of man's destruction of man. Just after the declaration of an independent Slovenian Republic in 1992, which was a parliamentary democracy, hundreds of thousands of people were "erased," that is, denied identity, their own history, passports, civil rights, subject to defamation, inequity, and humiliation. Dr. Anakiev was at this time a practicing medical doctor until he was added to the list of the "erased." Here, in the following poem, we have mention of Cerberus, the hell-hound of Hades, who keeps those who have passed through the River Styx (where memory is lost in the land of the dead), from passing into life again. Ironically, Dr. Anakiev equates the pseudo-democracy of Serbia with hell.

> Cerberus at the door
>
> of the Slovenian gulag
>
> is a democrat

Again, the author offers these remarks regarding the poem:

This poem expresses a very interesting idea related to democracy: just as in the case of The Trail of Tears, the contemporary case of the Slovenian Erased people is the result of illegal action by a legal democratic government. The legal government is breaking its own law in the name of democracy.

In the following poem, written before the outbreak of war in Yugoslavia, which had previously been a multi-cultural society, we see the suspicion of man towards man (and in this poem Dr. Anakiev uses a kigo of winter to good affect):

> the start of the war—
>
> Through bare branches I spy on
>
> my neighbors' houses

Here is the author's commentary:

The last two lines of the poem were written in Tolmin, Slovenia, in the winter of 1990 just before the Yugoslav war started. I was aware of the nationalistic excitation of my neighbors, but not being an ethnic Slovenian it had not made an impression on me.

To convey the unspeakable horror that resulted from the war in Yugoslavia, Dr. Anakiev transfers a human experience to nature, since the unspeakable is also the irrational. The short poem is based on Basho's famous poem

> The summer grasses—

163

Of brave soldiers' dreams

The aftermath.

Here is Dr. Anakiev's version

Young grasses...

A mountain bleeds from a helmet

full of dreams

One is reminded of the difficulty inherent in writing poetry after the Holocaust. As Theodore Adorno said ""to write poetry after Auschwitz is barbaric." For Adorno, no language, no poetry, could possibly begin to articulate the horror that had been unleashed upon the world. The inhumane cruelties of Auschwitz, Dachau, death marches, and crematoriums could never be contained in sonnet, villanelle, sprung rhythm, free verse. (Anaya M. Baker, cited in Poetry of the Holocaust: Writing After Auschwitz).

Additionally, the poem also refers to the WWI battles of the Isonzo which were fought around the Tolmin area where Dimitar lived.

To think that the horrors of the Balkan wars were only in the past is to delude oneself. The Balkans, as Dr. Anakiev has pointed out, is primarily rural, and in these rural areas, the far-right still thrives. There exists a primitivism in the rural lands, based highly on traditions, shared languages. The emphasis on tradition is aligned with anti-modernism. For the rustics, anti-intellectualism predominates, as reflection is seen as a form of emasculation. Disagreement is discouraged. There exists the fear of difference. Economic frustration proliferates. Xenophobia also predominates, as does envy of the wealthy.

These examples are but a few of what Umberto Eco outlined in his analysis of what he called Ur-Fascism (New York Review of Books, 1995).

One can visibly see these complexes in the rustic population throughout the Balkans through the eyes of Dr. Anakiev.

In the Balkans

at the calling out of "rustic"

swastikas sprout

The author notes:

> The Socialist Federal Republic of Yugoslavia was founded on the basis of fighting fascism during WW2. The democratic governments of national states in the Balkans were founded on the basis of a "goat's milk" philosophy. Many collaborators of the regimes of Hitler and Mussolini are politically rehabilitated only because they are "ours".

Visibly impressed by this poem, Kuniharu Shimizu drew a haiga and Ban'ya Natsuishi translated the poem into Japanese:

Na Balkanu   in the Balkans

u ime rustike   calling the name of rustic

cvetaju swastike   swastikas grow

バルカン諸国で田舎者の名を呼ぶと鉤十字育つ   translation by Ban'ya Natsuishi

Dimitar Anakiev (Slovenia)

artwork: Kuniharu Shimiziu

165

And, as a marginal note, Ban'ya Natsuishi shares Dr. Anakiev's distrust and anomie towards Western European and Anglo-American global domination. It is found in his poem:

> Put a period deeply
>
> into the desert
>
> at the center of the new world

As can be expected, Dr. Anakiev, savors his praise for those who promote a cross-culturalism, a non-nationalistic approach to poetry/haiku. Being marginalized himself for so many years, Dr. Anakiev relishes freedom and the banishment of rules that are imbalanced, that favor one of the forms in a binary opposition to the detriment of the other. Here are a few of his glowing words for Richard Gilbert's *Poems of Consciousness* (Redmoon Press, 2008):

Richard Gilbert's Poems of Consciousness represents the first voice in Anglo-American haiku criticism to bring to an international readership democracy instead of authority. This anti-dogmatic book tears down the prejudices which have been built up and culminated over decades of English-language haiku theory. In this work the genre is rescued from overly complex ideologies and refreshed by concepts inspired by simple and common poetic truths...

Let me also stress here: International haiku is not a name for a new concept in haiku but the result of democratic practice, which began its official life as a form of organization in the Tolmin Haiku Conference 2000, and has now found its theoretical footing in Gilbert's work, and its real home in the democratic haiku practice of the Kumamoto poetic circle. It is my great hope that the democratic practice of International haiku will become more influential, at both the national and international level. (A Gift Of Freedom: Interpenetration in Haiku, Anakiev, A Gift Of Freedom: Interpenetration in Haiku, 2008).

It is in the field of cultural struggles (and this is related to cultivation, as in husbandry) that the future holds political possibilities of a renewed Balkans. As Dr. Anakiev wrote:

> A big field of
>
> cultural struggle: hens
>
> are laying eggs again.

The author notes:

> Culture is the field of cultural struggle. Perhaps the only field still open for
> rebellion. Bertolt Brecht said: "A book is an armament, take it in your hands"
> and I think it still works.

And, it must be borne in mind that in the cultural struggle, Dr. Anakiev never
wields a sword, but always wields a pen/pencil: He is the witness to the death and
ongoing rebirth of the world:

> The capital
>
> of my heart: just one
>
> sharpened pencil

He is fully aware that this carries a burden, because the author must put all else
aside in focusing on the cultural struggle; he may sometimes have to depict cruelty,
horrors, without intervening.

> The idea for the poem came as a result of becoming conscious of the
> cruelty of the poet's job. To be a good writer or a good poet means making poetry
> and literature the most important thing in one's life. No compromise, merciless. A
> gladiator's job.

> Noting the war crimes committed by many involved in the breakdown of
> Yugoslavia, Dr. Anakiev gives us a sarcastic reminder of the pseudo-innocence of
> these war criminals.

> With souls full of goat's milk
>
> rustic heroes
>
> fill the jails

Recall that "rustics" has an encoded meaning and then consider the significance of
"goat's milk" as a cultural reference to the rustics' sense of tribal identity.

Our author comments on this poem:

> The Balkans is primarily rural. Even the people living in cities are the
> first urban generation.. many of today's urban Balkans suffer a nostalgia for their
> villages, like a paradise they have left., goat's milk is a metaphor for expressing

rustic nostalgia, especially for Montenegrins but for others as well. One often hears the phrase "I miss the goat's milk from my village." Our statesmen fabricate a "Goats milk story", and create a "Goat's milk nationalism". These people, even after completing their education, relate goat's milk to the center of their world. Often they don't understand problems of the modern world because they hate the modern world. One can imagine those accused of war crimes in the former Yugoslavia before the judges at the International Criminal Tribunal: "You bloody bastards, you never tasted goat's milk from my village, you have no right to judge my war activities..." Tasting the goat's milk from a mountain village signifies an initiation into Holy Nationalism in the Balkans. You do not need to actually try the milk, it's enough to say: "Yes, I know what you mean..." because the rustic Balkan soul suffers from not being understood in the centers of power. The "culture of goat's milk" is dying in the prisons of The Hague.

What we see in Dr. Anakiev's pencil is radical in the world of haiku. Dr. Anakiev challenges readers/writers of the form to engage in politics (since they are, wittingly or no, already situated so). Politics in haiku has long remained something of a taboo, at least if it is too direct, which has virtually eliminated conscious politics from entering its content. However, even when poets are seemingly "apolitical," writing is a social practice and hence a political process. To compose poems devoid of human nature is to void human nature; to present pictures of a "pristine" nature is to indulge in the delusion of a golden age (and remember America has a long history of being regarded, particularly by writers of the 19th Century, as the new Eden, freed from history).

Dr. Anakiev works in the tradition of the exponents of exposing the subterfuges of the hegemonic culture in his poetry. As Adrienne Rich wrote:

Poetry is neither an end in itself, nor a means to some external end. It's a human activity enmeshed with human existence; as James Scully names it, a social practice. Written where, when, how, by, for and to whomever, poetry dwells in a web of other social practices historically weighted with enormous imbalances of social power. To say this is not--as these essays vividly demonstrate--to deny the necessity for poetry as an art whose tangible medium is language.

It's a commonplace to say that in a society fraught with official lying, hyperbolic urgings to consume, contrived obsolescence of words (along and the people who produce them) poets must "recover" or "subvert" or "re-invent" language. Poetic language may thus get implicitly defined as autonomous terrain apart from the ripped-off or colonized languages of daily life.

It's an even older commonplace to claim "the imagination" as a kind of sacred turf. The appeal to a free-floating imagination permeates discussions of poetry and is traced to many honored sources from Coleridge to André Breton to Wallace Stevens to Barbara Guest. It can assume a degraded public world to which is opposed the poet's art as an activity-in-itself, distinct from other kinds of activity, work, production, save perhaps as metaphor. (Line Break: Poetry as Social Practice).

It may be tempting to describe the poetry of Dr. Anakiev as polemical, but it would be more apropos to describe it as paralyzing, as psychologically distressing, as a way of finding catharsis by gracing memory with a voice. The air is frozen around the entryway to Dr. Anakiev's psyche and only humanization came give it the warmth needed to dilute it.

> "When we were soldiers . . ."
>
> The refrain hangs in the frozen air
>
> of my entryway

The refrain, the repetition, is something like the symptom of post-traumatic stress disorder; the song is the song of the stuck in a repeated, painful time, however convivial it is portrayed in the above poem. To enter the world of Dr. Anakiev is to pass through the entryway of war and its gory grotesqueries.

Even in his descriptions of commonplaces, there are signs of the unnatural, a way of emphasizing the omnipresence of whatever is vilest in the history of the Balkans. In winter, we expect that flies will be gone, but for Dr. Anakiev the dead keep returning, even out of season, even out of time sequence. Even dead flies have an ominous connotation to them in his world, as if they are signs that nothing has normalized in his world. Even on New Year's Eve, the turning point in nature when evening and darkness begin to withdraw and cultures often celebrate the new strengthening of nature with fireworks and celebrations, Dr. Anakiev can only find more "gathering," not as a social ceremony of joy, but as a gathering of mass graves, upturned dead flies (so like humans in their death postures).

> New Year's Eve—
>
> the window still gathers

dead flies

Dimitar says of this poem:

In 1993 I left the army but my family and I were on different sides of the front. My wife and daughter were able to reach me travelling circuitously around Europe. We went to my father's mountain house on the Serbian-Bulgarian border to spend a few days together. The house had long been empty but the window sills were full of dead flies.

In *Rustic,* history and domination and death reach back further in time than the wars in Yugoslavia in the 1990s. Dr. Anakiev retreats backward in time when Germany dominated the entire region of Eastern and Western Europe in the following poem:

Mitteleuropa:

in the grey cloud

a shadow of death

Dimitar says: The political concept of Mitteleuropa was offered by Slovenian separatists in late '80s and the beginning of the '90s as an alternative to the political concept of Yugoslavia. The poetry festival "Vilenica" was founded to promote ideas of Mitteleuropa in contrast to the "pro-Yugoslav" concept of the world famous Macedonian poetry festival "Struga". One of the first laureates of the Valencia poetry festival was the Austria writer Peter Handke. He was asked in a press conference about Mitteleuropa, and he answered: " I have no idea about Mitteleuropa, for me Mitteleuropa is a place with a grey sky all the time..." I was traveling to Prague to receive the "Medal of Franz Kafka" and finding myself following grey clouds in the sky the whole time, I recalled the words of Peter Handke.

Mitteleuropa is also the German term equal to Central Europe. The word has political, geographic and cultural meaning. While it describes a geographical location, it also is the word denoting a political concept of a German-dominated and exploited Central European union that was put into motion during the First World War. The historian Jörg Brechtefeld describes 'Mitteleuropa' as the following:

The term 'Mitteleuropa' never has been merely a geographical term; it is also a political one, much as Europe, East and West, are terms that political scientists employ as synonyms for political ideas or concepts. Traditionally, Mitteleuropa has been that part of Europa between East and West. As profane as this may sound, this is probably the most precise definition of Mitteleuropa available. (J. Brechtefeld, Mitteleuropa and German politics. 1848 to the present (London 1996).

The Mitteleuropa plan was to achieve an economic and cultural hegemony over Central Europe by the German Empire and subsequent economic & financial exploitation of this region combined with direct annexations, settlement of German colonists, expulsion of non-Germans from annexed areas, and eventual Germanization of puppet states created as a buffer between Germany and Russia.

Dr. Anakiev is so acutely aware of the violent history of his cultural heritage and region that even in "grey clouds" he can see the signs of impending death and destruction. History, as Marx said, repeats itself, first as tragedy and then as farce. But, we find nothing farcical here.

Even where we expect signs of culture and the springs of life- in the digging of a well and in reaching a drop of water (that everlasting symbol of life), the digging also unearths the stratum, the archeology of death and murder.

> Drop of well water—
>
> gravediggers dig up
>
> my ancestral bone

Dr. Anakiev places this poem in the following context:

Drop of well water represents ancestry.

The village funeral of my father was at a mountain cemetery, without a priest, following an ancient ceremony led by the oldest villager. I have heard that this poem has something in common with the Celtic mythology. (Dimitar, as an Erased, couldn't travel and had lost contact with his parents and couldn't attend his father's funeral).

A man, as Dr. Anakiev knows, has yearnings for belonging to nature, to his society, to his family, to his culture, language, to all the usually unspoken needs of fulfilled citizens. But for Dr. Anakiev all of this was denied. In the following poignant poem, we see this unsated appeal in the following one line verse:

from the balcony unreachable mountains

Anakiev brings up for the first time in this poem the period when the Republic of Serbia, a democratic parliamentary state, "erased" members of its population.

Here is the context provided by the poet:

The balcony of my apartment in Tolmin was a symbol of my life for more than 10 years after I returned to independent Slovenia. To break with the Yugoslav policy of "brotherhood and unity" , and to foster enemies, the Slovenian government erased from the official records more than 25,000 people. All of the Erased, among them 6,000 children, instantly found themselves without any human rights: people of no-official-existence. Among them, me. Living without documents is not easy. Most of the time I spent on my balcony watching mountains.

Under the fallen sky

the freaks of chaos become

a hospitable sea

Here the unbearable is depicted as the impossible: a fallen sky. Naturally, the unnaturalness of this state of affairs is a "freak," and "chaos," the Greek word for lack of cosmos and order in the universe and society. Yet for some unknown reason, Dr. Anakiev compares this state of affairs to a "hospitable sea," something welcome if inhuman.

Dr. Anakiev discusses this as a mythological poem, one which reaches back through the turbulent history of the Balkans to the time of Alexander the Great and up through and to the present modern wars. He reminds us that "the hospitable sea" was a Greek euphemism for the Black Sea.

As Kirsten Fischer noted in her essay mentioned above (In the Beginning Was the Murder (Ibid):

Adorno's view of the civilization process is not, like Freud's, a tabooing of violence due to its first use against fellow man and following ritual enclosure. He rather suggests a removal of violence-taboos as the result of the use of violence against creatures. This violence became boundless by its ideological justification.

According to Adorno's reconstruction of the history of philosophy as natural history, aggression against nature is inevitably an artificial result of civilization's emergence from its origins. With this thesis Adorno refers to the psychic mechanism of projection discovered by Freud. In the course of the rationalization process aiming at the domination of nature, all uncivilized creatures are perceived as evil because of their incompatibility with sociocultural rationality...

Nature must contrast sharply with civilization and is perceived as evil as such; it must be exterminated to preserve civilization, and soon the self-preservation running wild has its dialectic set-back. Initially self-preservation by the domination of nature was an anthropological development which was both necessary and positive. Adorno agrees with Nietzsche's reminder to be grateful for the end of "continual fear of wild animals, of barbarians, of gods and of our own dreams" made possible by the rationalization process.7 The running wild of self-preservation as a regression of civilization into its former state and antithesis rather results from its ideological justification. This justification demonizes nature and therefore enables its unrestrained, exterminating domination. Adorno does not criticize the domination of nature as such but rather its boundlessness, which leads to its dialectical set-back. This set-back is a dialectical one because, according to Adorno, the absolute domination of nature provokes destructive socio-cultural phenomena, since the domination of fellow humans and the domination of nature are closely related through history in a disastrous way. They cannot be separated from each other.

We can easily see this unrestrained, reflex striving for survival and indifference to the slaughter of creatures in one of Dr. Anakiev's most well-known haiku:

> Spring evening.
>
> The wheel of a troop carrier
>
> crushes a lizard.

> Animal Day—

> lop-ears of a rabbit
>
> full of jumping light

The author has this to say about "Animal Day":

There is no "Animal Day," but I invented this holiday for out pet rabbit living in his prison on our inner balcony.

One cannot help but see the irony and ambivalence in this poem and commentary. While an animal ordinarily slaughtered and eaten is kept by the poet as a pet, he is caged and this is equated to keeping him in a "prison."

And, we can see how "alien" people are easily dominated by the hegemonic culture because of the association of them with nature and with pre-cultural existents: Dr. Anakiev gives us this poem, one that relates to the United States of America:

> A tomahawk made
>
> to forget its native tongue
>
> keeps the democracy

One does well here to recall Dr. Bruno Bettleheim's *The Informed Heart* (1960), where Dr. Bettleheim records his experiences as an inmate of a concentration camp during WWII and how he discovered that by maintaining his humane emotions as well as intellectual distinctions, he as well as those inmates who shared these values remained alive and morally intact, whereas those who strove to struggle to survive at any cost either died or lost what was most essential to their humanity: the human heart.

Bettleheim's view was that the individual's inner control of hostility was the key to interethnic harmony, while projecting hostility onto other social groups created the prejudicial attitude upon which the concentration camps were formed.

After all the suffering Dr. Anakiev underwent in the Republic of Serbia, from being a practicing medical doctor to suddenly become one of the "erased," I asked him how he bore it. He informed me that it was part of his maturation as a person and indirectly it forced him to learn a new language, that of film, and to become a successful and internationally known documentary and artistic director. It also formed his character to such an extent that he has spent the years of his life since

174

the wars in Yugoslavia writing haiku, forming haiku societies, documenting the lives and history of the various people who comprise the population of the Balkans. Some of his films are available online (all you need do is search under Anakiev films); some are with English subtitles and some are not. He has a unique way of juxtaposing and overlapping different historical periods, with old engravings, poems overlaying them, and always the faces and voices of people. People stand out in his works, poetic and filmic. This is his heritage and his inheritance, what he will leave to the world. The people in the films are not actors, but ordinary people, sometimes the very last living member of a long line of family genealogy.

In his poems, as is readily evident, there is a strong voice, a strong human presence, a man who takes a stand without following the "rules" and "taboos" laid down by Anglo-American and Western European haiku poets. If you recall his speech at the HNA of 2012, you will agree that there is a "capitalist haiku," one which in a sense dehumanizes mankind by removing him/her completely from the tabloid of words. These poems are not neutral, not innocuous, for they implicitly project a view of the insignificance of humanity.

I will close with words from Bruno Bettelheim, if only because Dr. Bettelheim went through as horrific and catastrophic an experience as did Dr. Anakiev.

Dr. Bettelheim (The Informed Heart) wrote in the preface:

With so much at hand that generations have striven for, how bewildering that the meaning of life should evade us. Freedoms we have, broader than ever before. But more than ever before most of us yearn for a self-realization that eludes us, while we abide restless in the midst of plenty. As we achieve freedom, we are frightened by social forces that seem to suffocate us, and that seem to move in on us from all parts of an ever contracting world.

As Karen Zelan wrote in her obituary essay *Bruno Bettleheim* (1903 to 1990, Prospects: the quarterly review of comparative education, (Paris, UNESCO: International Bureau of Education), vol. XXIII, no. 1/2, 1993, p. 85-100, ©UNESCO: International Bureau of Education, 2000):

To combat the unpredictable outcomes of our fast changing world, Bettelheim wrote that we can no longer afford to bifurcate the reasons of the heart from the reasons of the mind. 'The daring heart must invade reason with its own living warmth, even if the symmetry of reason must give way to admit love and the pulsation of life.'

Bettelheim never lost sight of the importance of feeling. Exquisitely educated in the history of reason, his life's work consisted of advising us to inform pure reason with the emotions, which is the very substance of a humanistic psychology.

These same words could easily be applied to the life and work of Dr. Dimitar Anakiev. He has left a living legacy of humanistic art for future generations to learn from and for that we owe him a great debt. His strong, personal voice is not just his own: it is the voice of man as a species-being, just as Marx described man, not as an isolated monad living only for self-fulfillment. Life is too dear for that.

The Potter's Wheel: Mark Truscott's *Nature*

On the back jacket of Mark Truscott's book Nature (BookThug, Toronto,2011), there appears the following quote:

Nature is us and we are nature. Nature is out to kill us. Nature is heterosexual. Nature is gay. Nature is masculine. Nature is a woman. Nature is natural. Nature is culture. Nature is the nature of reality. Nature is a metaphor. Nature is like money. Nature is calling. Few ideas today are as charged or subject to as many contradictory inflections as is nature.

With this understanding of the overly determined symbol/thing *Nature,* we find ourselves moving into territory that has been left unexplored in the world of haiku poetry for the past half-century. Mr. Truscott, merely in introducing the complexities of the subject of nature, advances our understanding multitudinously. For although we tend to think there is a consensus on what nature means or is, we neglect the fact that nature has a history, not just a natural one, but a semantic one, an ontological one.

Traditionally, haiku written in the Anglo-American world, has taken nature as its subject matter. While there are those who understood that the proper subject of haiku, as practiced by the Japanese originators of the form, was the seasons, which are man-made constructs and do not exist in nature *per se,* rather than merely nature, not a few of the haiku practitioners of the past fifty years have written solely on the topics of nature. And, they have done so as if nature were a given, something not an artifact, something "outside" rather than "inside," something we were separated from long ago, something we were torn from, from our own efforts to arrive at *culture.*

Of course, the Japanese, when they wrote haiku, used a *saijiki,* a compendium of seasonal words, animals, fauna, flora, with literary examples of previous poems on each subject listed; Japanese haiku was a literary-phenomenological constellation, with each new expression of the form bearing allusions to the cultural past. This was not and could not be the case in English, as there existed to equivalent to the *saijiki.* The result was more often than not flat, "objective" descriptions of nature or denoters of nature. The flatness was the consequence of there being no cultural/historical context for the poems; they were words on a page, mostly nouns, that were meant to produce at most a mood, a feeling; they could not evoke more.

The history of the idea of nature is an important one for anyone writing haiku. Nature, for instance, had as its initial meaning the "essential" quality of something. As Raymond Williams puts it in *"Ideas of Nature"* in *Problems in Materialism and Culture* (London, Verso, 1980):

> *The association and then the fusion of a name for the quality with a name for the things observed has a precise history. It is a central formation of idealist thought. What was being looked for in nature was an essential principle: The multiplicity of things, and of living processes, might then be mentally organized around a single essence or principle: a nature.*

Then, this singularizing of multiple processes found competition in the idea of God as the organizing and sole agency of meaning in the world. Briefly, by the Nineteenth Century and the strengthening of the sciences, the personified nature resumed its first principal position. As Raymond Williams pointedly remarks about the many versions of nature:

> *What is often being argued, it seems to me, in the idea of nature is the idea of man; and this not only generally, or in ultimate ways, but the idea of man in society, indeed the ideas of kinds of societies. For the fact that nature was made singular and abstract, and was personified, has at least this convenience: that it allows us to look, with unusual clarity, at some quite fundamental interpretations of all our experience. Nature may indeed be a single thing or a force or a principle, but then what these are has a real history.* (Ibid)

And with this bifurcation, we come to the "modern" view of man versus nature, as man and other, as Williams says:

> *It is now well enough known that as a species we grew in confidence in our desire and in our capacity to intervene. But we cannot understand this process, indeed cannot even describe it, until we are clear as to what the idea of nature includes, and in particular whether it includes man.*

> *For, of course, to speak of man 'intervening' in natural processes is to suppose that he might find it possible not to do so, or to decide not to do so. Nature has to be thought of, that is to say, as separate from man, before any question of intervention or command, and the method and ethics of either, can arise. And then, of course, this is what we can see happening, in the development of the idea. It may at first*

seem paradoxical, but what we can now call the more secular and more rational
ideas of nature depended on a new and very singular abstraction: the abstraction of
Man. It is not so much a change from a metaphysical to a naturalist view, though
that distinction has importance, as a change from one abstract notion to another,
and one very similar in form. (Ibid).

We do not have the time or space to investigate fully the subject of nature as
such. The above discussion is meant as a preamble to Mark Truscott's intricate,
minimalist poems that call, each in its own way, to us to question our assumptions
about the subject that as haiku poets we have for so long taken for granted.
Although he is not a haiku poet *per se,* he has acknowledged an indebtedness to the
form.

In the following poem, Mr. Truscott gives us reason to pause: is *Nature* a
single entity/process/cause with a single unifying principal as well as the name for
that thing, the essence, its nature, or is it something that cannot be considered
within the parameters of number (being a human construction of relations)? Is it
one or a non one? Or, is it alternatively the subject of adulation, as in "O," followed
by its unitary nature on no one, meaning nothing else exists "outside" of its fullness,
or is it the unity that exists on itself in the form of "on one," meaning man or being?

NATURE

one
or
a
non

one
o
one
on

no
one
on
one

Then, the question is posed by Mr. Truscott as to whether or not nature has a form and can that form be simulated, is it simulated, by and in language. Is language a part of nature or as a part of culture is it something *contra-naturum*, or, at the least, unmotivated, un-natural, a symbol of the symbol maker, the creator of divisions, discreet entities, but not merely another such one. The answer would seem simple enough, as language is an object in one sense, but is it man-made and world making or is it as sound, figure, nature. Mr. Truscott plays with language in answering this question:

FORM

These

two

words

We unquestionably have a form here, but it is invented, not two words, but three, and the pronoun these is equivocal; which two words is the poet referencing? Nonetheless, does this mean that it is not a natural form? Forms in nature are compounded, built up into greater or lesser extent and complexity by combination. There is nothing that is not compounded and so of words and language and what we do with them. If that is the case, how can form in say a poem not be a happening of nature?

Joining man and nature, or rather recognizing they are always and already like a möbius strip avoids the commodification, pollution, domination of nature that so haunted so many, including that great questioner of the dangers of humanism, Charles Olson. In "The Praises," as Craig Stormont points out in his essay *Charles Olson and the Nature of Destructive Humanism:*

Olson's critique of the unfounded elevation of the ego, or our opinion of ourselves in relation to other objects, resulted in his formulation of "objectism." Objectism is Olson's approach to experience, in which he suggests that in the hierarchy of the universe, man is no more important than a tree or a stone:

Objectism is the getting rid of the lyrical interference of the individual as ego, of the 'subject' and his soul, that

peculiar presumption by which western man has interposed himself between what he is as a creature of nature (with

certain   instructions to carry out) and those other creations of nature which we
may, with no derogation, call objects.

For a man himself is an object, whatever he may take to be his advantages, the
more likely to recognize himself as

such the greater his advantages, particularly at that moment that he achieves
an humilitas sufficient to make him of

use

Mark Truscott, however, is in no manner a destructive humanist. His poems belie such an interpretation. If anything, Mr. Truscott premises his poems on the foundation that all artifacts are part of nature and are natural. In the following poem he creates a balanced, concrete poem that again refuses to confine human configurations of relationships to humans, that is, outside of nature.

SQUARE

which is

which is

He has created as square with words and has proclaimed that it "is" and the copula is "existence," it links as nature links something with its processes. The repetition of "which is" makes the two or rather four sides of the poem equal in angularity and dimension, the whole a square, some *thing (Nature)*. Equal=Equivalent.

If anything, Mr. Truscott is not an evolutionist, is not a believer in progress, development, that nature and man have a teleology. Nature, including man, has no particular purpose or aim. As he says in one of his poems:

on and on toward and on

Process, movement, collapse, construct, human and nature go on, but the direction is undecided, indecipherable, just "and," additional "on," additional process. As the poet Charles Simic put it in *Walking the Black Cat* (Harcourt, 1996):

Everything is teetering on the edge of everything/with a polite smile

Although the following poem comes from Mr. Truscott's first book, *Said Like Reeds or Things* (Coach House Books, Toronto, 2004), it's a one word poem on the subject of nature, or, put otherwise is one word nature:

leaf

Poet and critic, Ron Silliman had this to say about it:

Is it conceivable that a nature poetry – for that's what this is, with Truscott very much being one to include language in his understanding of nature – this spare? To appreciate the one-word poem as poetry means to be able to see & hear the sensuality of soft consonants aligned with a pair of vowels that create a single, clear tone.

Nature functions by increase, always increase, always as the bard wrote, the procreant urge of the world. Nature is prolific; it is its way of guaranteeing that what is produced thrives and survives; seeds, eggs, dropped the moment after maturity to continue. For Mr. Truscott this is the "and" of nature; "and" is nature's way, "and is nature language. He says,

and and and and and this and

Nature doesn't discriminate in its function of multiplying, nor does the poet; "this"

can refer to anything; in the context, the specificity of the pronoun is unnamed and unknown; that is how it comes to fruition.

Mr. Truscott writes a similar poem, however in this poem he plays with the order of words and even uses the morpheme "s" to designate what it does for us: convey more, plurality.

if branches

s branch

If there are branche(s) then there are "s" branch; it is a unique way of arousing attention to our way of naturally increasing; it becomes something of a mnemonic device for the poet, as he uses individual sounds to convey meaning on more than this occasion.

A bird sings a

letter hangs in the balance

There is an indeterminacy created here, as the significance could be that a bird sings something like or similar to a letter and the bird or the sound hangs in the balance. But the poet doesn't say like, it isn't a metaphor, it is either "a" or "a letter," that the bird is heard to make and in either event we have not the personification of the non-human so much as the possibility of alternating the bird's sound with human sound, human speech, bird speech, in an event, a meaning. The balance described is that the first line begins and ends with the letter "a." Language does that or can do that; like nature it is capable of balance. There is parity in "a" and "a." There is also the enjambment and the difficulty of maintaining balance as the second "a" tilts its weight to the "letter" that it is. Meaning and nature are "hanging" here: this is balance.

Mark Truscott uses single letters in a number of other poems in *Nature.* They are sound things in each instance; objects of nature; the smallest bit of the larger alphabet, the human system, or one of them, to be; they are our gesticulations, gestures, phonemes, they combine and recombine like strands of DNA in multiple combinations, all with the joy, for lack of a better term, for of existence.

an n on

a door

It is not possible to parse this poem, in the sense of interpreting it in any kind of once and for all fashion. Perhaps, that is the reason the poet uses letters like an "n" on a door; the poem, like nature, remains to the end whatever we make of it; it is more than multiple meaning; for us meaning is essential, but for nature it is not. But both have entities, existing in each their own fashion. One could, if they chose, read this poem to be playing with anon, the most prolific writer in the history of literature. He figures from the beginning, but is completely unknown and unknowable. So many wise and beautiful thoughts have been attributed to anon that it would be fair to say he is "a door," the way to ancient life and wisdom. Or anon can refer to a later time, to time, to delay or deferring of meaning in language. Or, perhaps it is just what it says: an "n" on a door.

The a

sticks.

A the

on the

floor.

The letter "a" is the first, the primary letter of the alphabet; it has its origins in the Greek letter "alpha," which means the beginning and from which all else follows. It has religious overtones, as the Christian savior, coeval with God the Father, was the Alpha and Omega, the beginning and the end; everything and in between. Mr. Truscott doesn't tell us what it means, directly, but by attribution, that it "sticks," it takes on identity, that which "sticks," stays, remains. It is like matter in its way, the building block of the universe, as it is the third most used letter in the English language. From it so many combinations are possible, and it is only the beginning of endless permutation of *parole,* of individual utterance. "A" sticks because it has traveled so far. It is "aleph" of the Phoenician alphabet, and may have been the origin of latter historical letters, the "aleph" of the Hebrews and Arabs. The Etruscans brought it to the Italian Peninsula, and the Romans adopted it.

So when Mr. Truscott says the "A" the on the floor, he is talking about the foundation of the foundation that sticks and has stuck throughout history, natural and human and throughout their many valences and meanings. The "a" often means a mark of distinction, the highest grade, the best, and has even when used shown to have a motivating factor in human behavior and action.

air

around

rings

around

from

around

hills

around

    If any poem in the collection **Nature** has something of a life of its own, has a natural tone, it is this one. If any poem in the collection can be compared to a möbius strip, it is this one. The most common thing, air, atmosphere of nature/man, is around, rings around, from where, from around (it is the equivalent of omnipresent) hills or anything else that is "around." The poem circles itself, can be read top to bottom as well as from bottom to top. It is a word, around, but it is our place, our home, our sustenance, it is nature and it is around, around, around. In a poem of eight words, it is repeated four times; it is at least half of our existence air that is "around."

    As I promised the author, as the book is short, I would not include all the poems in the collection in this essay. I think we have seen enough of the poems to have a greater understanding of what Mark Truscott means by nature. As he said, it is us, it is like "money," insofar as it is the universal sign of value and inter-changeability. It can be exchanged or represent anything and it does and it works. Language for Mark Truscott is nature, too, an object, a sound, a presence, a reliance on an absence, a turning, a figuring, a figure. In such few words, Mark Truscott contains the world (which is the human).

Jouissance: The Poetic Achievement of Fay Aoyagi

That we live in a post-industrial, post-modernist age is long settled. That ours is an age of the advancement and transformation of information and its retrieval is uncontested. It was Jean Francois Lyotard who first coined the term **post-modernism** and his position was that any knowledge that could be adapted to translation into quantities of information and computerization would survive, and that knowledge that could not be so channeled, knowledge for its own sake, would be abandoned. He noted:

We may thus expect a thorough exteriorization of knowledge with respect to the "knower," at whatever point he or she may occupy in the knowledge process. The old principle that the acquisition of knowledge is indissociable from the training (Bildung) of minds, or even of individuals, is becoming obsolete and will become ever more so. The relationships of the suppliers and users of knowledge to the knowledge they supply and use is now tending, and will increasingly tend, to assume the form already taken by the relationship of commodity producers and consumers to the commodities they produce and consume – that is, the form of value. Knowledge is and will be produced in order to be sold; it is and will be consumed in order to be valorized in a new production; in both cases, the goal is exchange.

Knowledge ceases to be an end in itself; it loses its "use-value." (The Post-Modern Condition, Manchester University Press, 1984).

Poetry, certainly since the end of didacticism, has been a socially marginalized activity, existing for the most part in institutions. Mainstream poets have garnered some attention in the modern age, but certainly not as conveyers of information, of knowledge as understood by Lyotard. Haiku, as a poetic form, has been even more alienated from a broad readership than its mainstream equivalents. Poetry, including haiku, has for a long time relinquished exchange value.

Faced with the proliferation of knowledge in post-modernism and the subjugation of the subject as a mere nodal point through which pass the signs and codes of the social order and its priorities, poetry has taken, at minimum, two paths. The first is to appropriate the information of the computer age (called "flarf," where modern poets stitch together poems from the fragments of narratives found on the internet along with their own words), and what the critic Jennifer Ashton calls the "new imperatives to construct poems that appear to resist artifice, whether in the form of a commitment to sincerity, a lack of irony, a childlike innocence or wonder, artlessness, etc." (Sincerity and the Second Person: Lyric after Language Poetry, Interval (le) s II.2-III.1 (fall 2008/Winter 2009).

Unwrapping a package containing Fay Aoyagi's latest book, **_Beyond the Reach of My Chopsticks,_** I found myself beset by a bundle of signifiers. The cover painting/drawing by Chiyo Miyashita was done in soft pastel colors and intentionally reproduced the effect of childlike composition; it lacked dimension, its houses were placed on a curve rather than a flat surface to suggest the shape of the earth, the houses themselves-their windows- appeared to have faces, the sky was green, and the reflections of the houses in yellow water (without ripples or other signs of embodiment) did not always match the "original" houses. I stress that the "innocence" of the cover art is intentional, because Ms. Miyashita studied painting at the university level in Tokyo and is a sophisticated artist.

The title of the book suggested a state of loss, of what could not be grasped (a state of infancy insofar as the world referred to was unreachable, unmanageable), of a world beyond the narrator's reach, perhaps also of what was foreign and could not be appropriated (Fay Aoyagi emigrated to America in 1982 and began writing haiku in English in 1995). Before reading the poems, I suspected that Ms. Aoyagi had adopted the persona of the "eternal girl," the _puela aerterna_ in Jungian parlance. It seemed that Ms. Aoyagi was engaging in the new "innocence," with the aim of preserving the subject (assailed as an existent throughout the post-modern age) as a viable voice in poetics.

I was eager to see if Ms. Aoyagi referred, as she often does, to signifiers of her new country, a kind of "fluffing," an inter-textualizing of the Other. She had demonstrated this tendency in past references in her poems to Dylan, to laundromats, to a banjo, canned soup, RSVP, Independence Day, Pearl Harbor Day, Oscar night, and other American cultural signs.

Opening the book, I was not disappointed: the first poem represents the author's encounter with a mental image of an idea (what we call a word) that holds part of the Real, but not a very satisfactory part of it.

cauliflower-

another day without

an adventure

What can be more mundane, tasteless, without savor, than the idea of cauliflower? But, the author knows that when a signifier (cauliflower, in this case) becomes attached to a morsel of reality, something of the Real eludes capture. For "everything that comes into our field of recognition by means of a signifier, something of it must remain imperceptible, unsymbolized. This is the Real." (Lacan, A Beginner's Guide, Lionel Bailly, Oneworld Publications, 2009). Hence, the narrator's dissatisfaction. She is looking for the Real, and this requires "an adventure," and risk taking is one of the qualities associated with the *puela aeterna* in her search for completion and maturation.

The second poem in the collection gives the book its title and is quintessentially of loss and nameless desire:

low winter moon

just beyond the reach

of my chopsticks

Of course, the poem is not enclosed; there are multiple ways to read it. The low moon resembles a grain of rice or a sushi roll and the author plays with the fact that by perception it appears just beyond the grasp of her chopsticks. The ensemble of words may also refer to what exists just beyond her Japanese utensils, the world of the Other, as she is now in America, a foreign country. However, most compellingly, the low moon is the acoustic mental image of what Freud and then Jacques Lacan called *The Thing*: it is the object per se of loss, which attracts desire, although it is not itself the object of desire. "For Lacan, the Thing exists outside of language and the Symbolic- it is 'the first thing that separated itself from everything the subject began to name and articulate'" (Ibid).

In her quest for wholeness, Ms. Aoyagi follows the path, the language of the unconscious. We see it in the poems' metaphors, as the unconscious, structured as language, often uses condensation, the joining of other ideas of things to produce a new idea.

who will write

my obituary?

winter persimmon

Or, in this darker identification of the author:

inside of me

a silkworm

spits out the night

In these poems we can see the identification of the "ego," the objectifying of the ego with a withering persimmon (death) and with a silkworm that instead of spitting out silk spits out the night (death/sensuality). They are both powerful, beautiful poems and suggest that it is not merely the ego speaking [but the Subject (the self) as well.] With the first awareness of oneself as an identity, a unity, comes awareness of oneself as an object, too, so that the self is split. And, in a sense, the attributions one makes of this objectified "identity," are factitious; they exist in the Imaginary, the psychic realm where a story begins to unfold of who one is, through the eyes of others and oneself. As Ms. Aoyagi acknowledges, her past, her childhood was an experience of both beauty and unexpected pain, a split:

thorns of roses

I fold my past

in half

Yet, Fay Aoyagi, a woman warrior of the interior landscape, returns to where she can find the Self (beyond the Imaginary ego):

shroud of moss

I step into the land

of the ancient tales

To a covering that is usually associated with death and with the dark, Fay Aoyagi willingly leaves the "ordinary" behind and travels to the source of self, to the land of *mythos*, where signs and symbols and narratives will aid her in her quest for authenticity, for the stature of a true Subject (and not an imaginary ego). She goes back and deep into the psychic realms.

189

In the next section of the book, Ms. Aoyagi continues to allow her unconscious to speak. We find this through her use of signifiers without definite signifieds (the acoustic idea and our thoughts of the meaning of the idea), where a chain of signifiers produces "childlike" comparisons and understandings of the world. Saying this, on the other hand, does not preclude the conscious intention of the author; actually, she is quite conscious of her art; it is, as it were, the persona of innocence that she adopts.

There are a series of poems in this section that use the rhetorical form *metalepsis;* this figure of speech produces a transgression of the boundaries between distinct worlds and thus suggests awe and wonder (and fear and laughter).

> rumble of the metro
>
> a queue of city crabs
>
> inches forward

> slow ceiling fan
>
> a town hall meeting
>
> of the pet shop goldfish

> handcuffed lobsters
>
> in the water tank
>
> A-bomb Anniversary

The same transposition of realms noted above is related by the author to herself, thereby creating categorical confusion and further influences and modalities of the unconscious:

> summer's end
>
> I trade by wings
>
> for fins

The *aporia* of identity, the transformation of a human being into a bird and then a fish, highlights the Imaginary, simultaneously leaving traces of a Self/Subject beyond the confines of the fictional nature of the ego. It is both. In a world of objects, we are objects, and the Ideal identity is shared with other entities. It is the realm of the unaccountable, the Symbolic, where beings of the mind leave traces of existence in the mud of the Real:

> spring mud
>
> I find a comb
>
> left by a nymph

Most tellingly, the beings and objects of the world remind us of our first loss, the loss that initiates the quest for identity: the dyadic relationship to the mother, who is identical to the child in its beginning, who once lost is forever sought by means of following where she herself went to find fulfillment and wholeness and meaning (the name of the Father-the law of the world and its order and power). Here familiar sounds from nature are a path backward to the dyad.

> stepping stones
>
> the cicada chorus pushes me
>
> into Mother's house

Fay Aoyagi returns to this theme of the original relationship to the mother in the next section of the book. The ocean, for Carl Jung, was the embodiment of the unconscious, the mother from which consciousness is born, the womb of all being, and the French word for mother, *mere,* is a homonym for *mare,* the Latin word for the sea. It is a sea within, powerful, emotional, lively, without direction or security:

> inner ocean
>
> where a compass doesn't work
>
> winter rain

In keeping with the childlike relationship of the dyad, Ms. Aoyagi again takes on the persona of the naïve, innocent, and in this case she includes inter-textualization:

> tea garden

> the Dr. Dolittle in me
>
> whispers to a turtle

Just as Hugh Lofting, the author of Dr. Dolittle, had his character shun human beings and speak in the language of animals-a response of the author to the atrocities he saw in the trenches in WWI-so, Ms. Aoyagi, living in the modern world fraught with horrors, transforms herself into a version of Dr. Dolittle.

She gives us insight into what the horrors are that direct her to the imaginary world of literature in the following poem:

> Nagasaki Anniversary
>
> the constellation
>
> we never see from here

The constellation is that mushroom cloud that killed seventy-thousand people immediately and seventy-thousand later due to disease and radiation. It is something not recognized "here" in America (although it is, of course, taught in schools).

In the last poem of this section of the book, Fay Aoyagi, for the first time, insinuates herself, albeit in the third person, as in control, as an adult with the will and freedom to choose just how she will live, what she will hold on to and let go of: it is an important moment in the book.

> in the pool
>
> she sheds everything
>
> she wants to shed

In the next section of the book, Fay Aoyagi returns to the scenes of childhood, memory and deeply felt yearnings for something lost that is unspecified. There are amongst the poems here some achingly beautiful identifications with the small other (Lacan's *le petit autre* as well as the Other (Lacan's le grand autre). In the dark, opacity of a perhaps partially frozen lake, she sees a passage to the past: it is like a Rorschach upon which she can project whatever she wishes:

> icy rain-
>
> at the bottom of the lake

a door to yesterday

In the beauty of apple blossoms, she finds the desire to aspire to fly, to participate in the Other, all that which is of the order that predates her existence and is exterior to her; it is a place where all things are stored; it is omnipresent.

apple blossoms

the highest bidder

for my wings

Interestingly, Fay Aoyagi herself, in an essay titled *Dissection of the Haiku Tradition: Inner Landscape* (cited in Modern Haiku 40:2, 2009), discusses being an expatriate and feeling the need to fill a hole in herself: she also discusses being a winged creature:

Subconsciously, I may need a thing to fill a hole in my soul. I think haiku is helping me to do this. I still want to be a creature with wings rather than a stationary plant. But I do not want to be a mosquito anymore. I would like to avoid being slapped and killed easily. It does not mean I am clinging to life. Because I am involved with haiku, my senses have sharpened. I hope I can sharpen them more by exploring life through haiku.

Here are further examples of poems with a strain of longing for the past, or, something in the past that may hold the answer to the hole in her soul.

my yearning to spend a night inside a tulip magnolia

trailing an inchworm to a childhood summer

And, perhaps, the most beautiful poem in the collection, with its associative relation between shapes and space, the metonymical aspect of dream work and the unconscious discourse

a hierarchy of apples in moonlight

In the following section of the book, Ms. Aoyagi refers to a pastel-colored day, which reinstitutes the book jacket and its pastel appearance. And, in the poem she

193

deliberately uses a word- password-to refer to the means of entry into the world within things, the means whereby we find passage beyond ourselves into the *grand autre.*

> pastel-colored day
>
> a password
>
> for the budding willow

It is the metonymic of qualities, here softness, delicacy, in discourse that allows us access to fulfill desire, to initiate desire.

Insofar as the unconscious is structured and performs as language, it is synonymy of meaning that attracts love/eros to what is not strictly speaking a part object of a particular drive and function, yet institutes desire. In the poem below, we experience not only a love for the ocean, but a love for whatever is boundless, forever; a love that is never satisfied for an unattainable, uncircumscribed object:

> a "forever stamp" on a letter to the ocean

There are moments when Fay Aoyagi sexualizes desire. It is a stage of development of a full human being that cannot be forestalled or forbidden. The fact that these moments are "slight" points to the fact that love and desire often do not cohabitate and there is rarely, if ever, a rapport.

The ease with which the desire for love and sexual desire become intertwined and the possibilities for misunderstandings to arise are encapsulated in the very genesis of both things. The demands possible in both cases are almost bound to create confusion- the first, because it can only be answered in the fulfillment of the 'extra' of the demand (the effort put into making a really good meal, rather than just one that will quell hunger), and the second because as there is no justifiable need attached to the demand-why should it be answered, except as a proof of love? It is not uncommon that it is the 'giver' of the sexual favor who is in search of love rather than the recipient, and unless there is perfectly matched lust on both sides, there is almost bound to be disappointment. (Lacan: A Beginner's Guide, Ibid, pg. 144-5).

Furthermore:

The individual man and the individual woman in a joint sexual act are each pursuing a form of enjoyment that is distinct from and irrelevant to the other's: the object of the man is different from the object of the woman. (Ibid, pg. 151-2).

194

Here are some examples from Ms. Aoyagi's poems:

> Independence Day
>
> I let him touch
>
> a little bit of me

> unexpected pregnancy
>
> she spits out
>
> watermelon seeds

> a hole in my sweater
>
> I ask him one more time
>
> what he meant

As time passes, Ms. Aoyagi develops, matures into an awareness not only of the importance of existents other than her own, but to the fact that loss is ineluctable, that memory sustains, that "selves" that once were are now recognized as merely masks, personas of the ego, and not the real Subject/Self.

> these stones
>
> with a story inside-
>
> autumn deepens

> Valentine's Day
>
> how many ghosts
>
> do I keep in the hat box?

> Halloween-

I dress as the self

I left somewhere

Further, there is a sense of history developed in the author, one that has already been recognized, but now more aware of the world pre-existing her and its storms and unmentionable horrors. In the following poem, Ms. Aoyagi gives us a vivid, moving image of the atom bomb shadows of Hiroshima and Nagasaki:

Hiroshima Day-

I lean into the heat

Of the stone wall

It is through the unstated that the power of the stated appears; the understatement detonates the unseen facts.

Finally, for the mere joy of it, my favorite poem of Ms. Aoyagi's:

Ants out of a hole-

When did I stop playing

The red toy piano?

There is a spring *kigo* here in ants and this may have some bearing on the tiny, unturned sound of a toy piano. On the other hand, there is the line of red ants and the red piano with its line of keys that connects the images to form a whole. Whatever it is, it is the smallness and the wonder of tininess of ants and children and toys that combine to set the poem apart and make of it a petite object of desire.

In the end, Fay Aoyagi manages through her fulfillment as a poet to reach maturation, wholeness, and joy. The fantasies of childhood though they remain as a part of her are no longer the whole of her. Though some things are unattainable, she has reached what Jacques Lacan called *jouissance,* which is the enjoyment and usage of not attaining a goal, but a form of enjoyment derived from the usage of something in its legitimate (intended) way- the pleasure that comes with the functioning of the physical or psychological apparatus associated with a drive. It is a pleasure that is much more than one that eases a tension. It is completion. She has spoken her Self as Subject. Nothing more needs to be done.

Jack Galmitz began writing haiku in 1999. Awards and Other Honors: Intermittently, some of my poems have been chosen to appear in the annual anthologies published by Red Moon Press, and I was selected as one of the featured poets for A New Resonance 4: Emerging Voices in English-Language Haiku (Red Moon Press, 2005). In 2006, I was awarded the Ginyu Prize (chosen as the most accomplished books of haiku by the World Haiku Association) for my first two collections, A New Hand and Driftwood. I have sparsely written critiques of some haiku collections - the works of Tateo Fukutomi and the collection of Ban'ya Natsuishi's poems in A Future Waterfall. In 2010, I was awarded the Kusamakura Grand Prize in the foreign language category. I received a Runner-up award in the newly-inaugurated Vladimir Devidé Haiku Awards (2011). Two of my haiku received a Zatuei (Haiku of Merit) Award in the Vanguard category (World Haiku Review, December 2011). I have recently been named "contributing editor" at Roadrunner Haiku Journal. I have been honored to have been chosen to be an Associate of The Haiku Foundation, created by Jim Kacian.

Books Published: A New Hand (Wasteland Press, 2006); Driftwood (Wasteland Press, 2007); Za vrabec/For a Sparrow: Haiku [Translations into Macedonian by Igor Isakovski] (Skopje, Macedonia: Blesok, 2007, in Macedonian and English]; Balanced is the Rose (Wasteland Press, 2008); The Effects of Light (AHA Online Books, 2002); Of All the Things (Ascent Aspirations Publishing); Sky Theatre (Ink: Literary E-Zine); A Simple Circle & Rockdove (Traveling Forms: Japanese/English Haiku); and The Coincidence of Stars [ed., Chris Gordon] (ant ant ant ant ant, 2011); yards & lots (West Virginia, Middle Island Press, 2012).

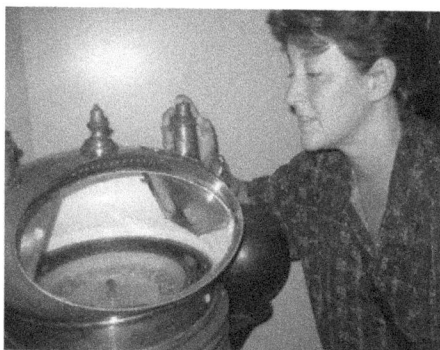

Beth Vieira is a student of Zen, haiku, and Japanese. She received her PhD from Johns Hopkins University in Comparative Literature and Intellectual History. She was a professor at the University of California at Berkeley before resigning to pursue a career as a psychotherapist. She has published in *Simply Haiku, Contemporary Haibun,* and *The Heron's Nest.* She has an essay on haiku in the journal *fort da* and a book length collection of poetry in the anthology *Burning Gorgeous.* She lives in Santa Cruz, California, USA, where she spends much of her time with her first love, the sea.

www.ingramcontent.com/pod-product-compliance
Lightning Source LLC
Chambersburg PA
CBHW020855090426
42736CB00008B/379